TORN HEART

Torn Heart

A Journey Through Trauma, Truth, and Transformation

Tara Benoit

©2025 All Rights Reserved. No portion of this book may be reproduced, stored in a retrieval system, or transmitted in any form or by any means—electronic, mechanical, photocopy, recording, scanning, or other—except for brief quotations in critical reviews or articles without the prior permission of the author.

Published by Game Changer Publishing

Paperback ISBN: 978-1-969372-48-3
Hardcover ISBN: 978-1-969372-49-0
Digital ISBN: 978-1-969372-52-0

Cover and author photographs © 2025 Rebekah Kay Photography

www.GameChangerPublishing.com

This book is for you—

For anyone who's faced a battle they didn't think they could survive.

For those who've been stuck in dark, tormented places where hope felt just out of reach. You can not only survive—you can rise.
I know, because I've lived it.

To my parents—thank you for showing me what strength, grace, and unconditional love look like.

To my husband, Jack— my partner through it all, and the one who gives me the absolute best belly laughs.

To Maximus and Magnus—my greatest reason, my brightest light. You are my heart.

To my sister, Sarah, and my brother, David—fellow warriors who faced their own pain and chose healing. I stand beside you, always.

To the doctors who believed me—thank you for giving my story space to be heard.

And to every SCAD survivor still learning how to live in a body that broke without warning… this is for you, too.

BEFORE YOU BEGIN

Thank you for being here and for stepping into my story.

The *Torn Heart Companion Workbook* was created to walk alongside you as you read—giving you space to pause, reflect, and make the journey your own.

Scan the QR code to get your copy.

Torn Heart

A Journey Through Trauma, Truth, and Transformation

TARA BENOIT

Foreword

An Invitation to Begin—Amberly Lago

When I first met Tara, I felt an instant spark—one of those rare connections where you just know someone is special. Her spunk drew me in, her heart inspired me, and her passion left me in awe. But what moved me most was her mission: to share her experience, her strength, and her hope in a way that doesn't just comfort—it awakens. Tara tells her story to stir something deep inside you, to call you out of silence, and to remind you that the very places you thought would break you can become the very ground where you rise stronger.

What you'll find in these pages is not a glossy story of overcoming, but an honest account of what it means to live through pain you didn't choose. For Tara, the struggle showed up in many forms—body image battles, buried memories, anxiety, depression, even moments when her own body threatened to betray her completely. On the outside, she wore resilience well. But on the inside, she was fighting for air, fighting to belong, fighting to believe she was enough.

And then came a moment that could have taken everything. An uncommon heart attack (SCAD)—sudden, terrifying, and almost dismissed—became another turning point in her journey. Doctors said she was fine, but her body knew otherwise. This part of her story stopped me in my tracks, because it reveals the quiet truth so many women know: our pain is often minimized, overlooked, or misunderstood. Tara's courage to keep pressing for answers, to advocate for herself when others didn't listen, is the same courage she now extends to you through these words.

She learned to listen when her body whispered, even when the world told her to quiet down. She leaned into movement, motherhood, and faith as anchors when the storm threatened to take her under. She discovered the power of telling the truth—first to herself, and then out loud—so the weight of it no longer crushed her in silence.

This book is so powerful because it doesn't just invite you to witness her healing; it gives you permission to begin your own. You'll recognize yourself in the moments of shame, of striving, of pretending everything's fine when it's not. But you'll also be reminded that there is another way. A gentler way. One where your body becomes an ally, not an enemy. One where your story becomes a bridge, not a burden. One where joy is possible—not because life is easy, but because you've chosen to keep showing up.

Tara's words carry both grit and grace. She offers them not as answers, but as a companion for the road. If you let them, they'll help you soften your gaze in the mirror, breathe more deeply into your own story, and find hope where you thought there was none left.

Reading this book feels like sitting with a friend who sees past your smile, who reminds you you're not too much and you're not alone. That's the gift Tara gives. And that's why I'm so honored to introduce you to her story.

If you've ever felt like you were meant for more, but fear or pain kept you playing small, let this book be your invitation to rise. If you've been waiting for the right moment to rise, to speak, to live fully—this is it. Tara's story is proof that no matter what you've walked through, no matter how broken you've felt, you can create a life of strength, freedom, and joy.

This is the book I wish I had when I was struggling and felt so alone. Turn the page with an open heart and step into the life you were created to live. Your transformation begins here.

—Amberly Lago, USA Today Bestselling Author, TEDx Speaker, Top 1% Podcast Host, Coach

Author's Note

I am beyond grateful that you chose to walk this journey with me.

This isn't just my story. It's a mirror for yours. If you've ever felt broken, unseen, or convinced your strength had slipped away—this book is for you.

My journey is unique, but the transformation is universal. Your path may look different, yet healing is still possible.

Whether you've faced illness, heartbreak, trauma, or the quiet battles no one else can see—I hope you find yourself in these pages. And may you feel your strength begin to return.

This book is here to remind you:
You are not alone.
You are never too broken to rise.
And your comeback can be more beautiful than you ever imagined.

I'm with you, every heartbeat of the way.

With love and light,
Tara Benoit

Contents

Foreword – An Invitation to Begin, by Amberly Lago — ix
Author's Note — xiii
Prologue – The Day My Heart Broke Differently — xvii

Part One – Foundations — 1
   Chapter 1 – You Are Just Big-Boned — 3
   Chapter 2 – The Pieces That Didn't Fit — 17
   Chapter 3 – Muscle, Motherhood, and the Pro Dream — 33
   Chapter 4 – The Day My Body Screamed — 45

Part Two – The Turning Point — 57
   Chapter 5 – SCAD – The Unexpected Heart Attack — 59
   Chapter 6 – The Fight to Be Seen — 69
   Chapter 7 – The List That Broke Me — 81
   Chapter 8 – When Recovery Isn't Linear — 89

Part Three – Rebuilding — 103
   Chapter 9 – The Brave Kind of Stillness — 105
   Heart Truths We Can't Ignore — 126
   Chapter 10 – Born from the Break — 129
   Chapter 11 – The Bridge No One Sees — 139
   Chapter 12 – The M.O.V.E. Method™ — 151
   Chapter 13 – The M.O.V.E. Compass — 175

Part Four – Becoming — 183
   Chapter 14 – When the Heart Ignites — 185

Chapter 15 – The Truth About Transformation … 201
Chapter 16 – A Love Letter to the Reader … 205
Chapter 17 – This Is Your Permission Slip … 207
Chapter 18 – Uncontrollably in Control … 209
Chapter 19 – Comfort Zones—The Edge of Becoming … 215

Epilogue – Forever Rising Higher … 219

Afterword – Doctors Who Walked Beside Me … 223

Beyond The Story … 227
   SCAD – The Beat That Remains … 229
   What the World Needs Now … 233
   I See You … 235
   Your Next Step … 239
   Heart Health Fact Sheet … 241
   Resources for Healing and Hope … 245
   Stay Connected … 249
   Acknowledgments … 251

Prologue

The Day My Heart Broke Differently

"And the day came when the risk to remain tight in a bud was more painful than the risk it took to blossom."
–Anaïs Nin

It wasn't supposed to happen to someone like me—fit, strong, unbreakable.

It started with a lightning bolt in my chest.

I thought it was a fluke—a pulled muscle. Body aches, maybe. But it wasn't.

I had just returned home from a vacation with my family, and days later, I came down with COVID. For two weeks, I was exhausted—down, and stuck in a haze.

But then, just as I was starting to feel better, I was lying in bed one night when something electric ripped through the left side of my chest. It wasn't like anything I'd felt before. Not a twinge. Not a cramp. A lightning strike—sharp, jarring, and unforgettable.

It came again. And again. Five to ten minutes of this strange, stabbing sensation, and then… nothing.

I told my husband, Jack. I told my mom. We all agreed to just watch and wait. That's what we do, right? We wait. We downplay. We rationalize.

Days later, I was getting my two boys ready for school—Maximus and Magnus, five and seven at the time. Yes, I know—we named them like a gladiator duo. We were upstairs in their bedrooms, the usual morning chaos unfolding—backpacks half-packed, pajamas scattered across the floor, and, of course, they had missed the bus. So, I was driving them in that day.

I bent down to put socks on one of them while the other was climbing on my back, full of energy and mischief, treating me like his personal jungle gym. That's when it started—a strange tingling in my left fingertips. The sensation traveled up my hand, my arm, and into my chest. My breath caught. A deep, aching squeeze gripped my heart, as if unseen hands were holding it too tightly. My neck ached. My jaw tightened.

Something was wrong. Deep down, I knew.

But I didn't want to scare my boys. They were smiling, laughing, and goofing off as kids do. I was terrified. But I didn't want them to know anything was wrong, so I drove them to school. Smiling. Functioning. Pretending. I glanced at them in the rearview mirror—giggling, carefree, still in that sweet in-between age where the world is magic. I couldn't let them see me unravel. So I swallowed the fear and kept my smile steady.

Only after I dropped them off did I call my mom. "I need you to take me to the ER. Something is wrong."

They took me in right away—young woman, chest pain, post-COVID—a quick triage. But after hours of bloodwork and basic tests, they told me

I was fine. Maybe it was anxiety, they said. Or maybe from the COVID recovery. And they sent me home.

I remember walking out into the parking lot, the fluorescent lights of the hospital behind me, my chest still aching. I felt invisible. Like I had spoken a language they didn't understand. Like maybe I didn't even understand it myself. But deep down, I knew—something was very, very wrong.

I walked out of that ER with the same pain in the left side of my chest I walked in with, but now I carried something heavier: doubt. They didn't believe me. Maybe I shouldn't either. Maybe I was being dramatic. Was I imagining it?

But I wasn't. I couldn't be. The ache was still there, constant and quiet like a warning I didn't yet know how to interpret. I could feel my heart. This was a strange feeling. But I couldn't shake the sense that something had changed—subtle, but enough to make the familiar feel unfamiliar.

The pressure in my chest never went away. I left the hospital on a Friday—still uncomfortable, still unsure. On Saturday night, I woke up with a sharp, stabbing pain shooting across my upper back. I got out of bed to find some Advil, hoping it might help.

My French bulldog, Moose, followed me back to my bedroom—something he never did at night. I let him curl up beside me, which was rare back then. After about an hour of tossing and turning, I finally drifted back to sleep.

Then came Sunday morning.

I wanted so badly to believe I was okay. That the doctors had been right. That I could stretch it out, breathe it away, carry on.

But I couldn't. Because deep down, I knew something wasn't right. My chest was heavy. My heart felt off. Like it was whispering something urgent that no one else could hear.

What was happening in my body was very real. It took six days from the onset of the first symptom, two ambulance rides, and two ERs before I would learn I'd experienced a rare heart event—something most doctors miss, especially in women. I wasn't having a panic attack. I wasn't just "recovering from COVID." I was in danger.

This was the beginning of everything unraveling… and everything awakening.

I didn't know it then, but that day would split my life into two parts: the woman I was before, and the woman I had to become.

♡ From My Heart to Yours

If you've ever had that quiet knowing in your body—that whisper that says *something's not right*—I want you to know this: you are not crazy, you are not dramatic, and you are not alone.

Pain that doesn't show up on a test is still real. Fear behind a smile is still fear. And sometimes the strongest thing you can do is keep going *and* speak up.

I didn't have all the answers in that moment. I didn't even have the language. But I had the truth inside me—and that was enough to begin.

Whatever you're facing, I hope you keep listening to your body. Keep asking questions. Keep choosing belief—especially when others don't.

This was the start of my unraveling.

But it was also the beginning of my becoming.

And so is yours.

PART ONE

FOUNDATIONS

The Roots We Bury
The Truths We Carry
The Pieces That Shape Us Before We Even Know

CHAPTER 1

You Are Just Big-Boned

"We delight in the beauty of the butterfly, but rarely admit the changes it has gone through to achieve that beauty."
–Maya Angelou

The Hunger for Control

The paper on the exam table crinkled beneath me. I was 15, legs swinging, heart pounding, trying to act casual as the doctor walked in. I had barely eaten that day—just water and gum—and I was proud of it. That meant control. That meant I was winning.

But I was starving myself.

When I finally landed at that annual physical, I remember dreading the scale. Could I take off my shoes? Why couldn't we have gone in the morning so I'd weigh less? Can I turn around so I don't see? It sounds silly now, but back then, the number determined everything.

I had lost a significant amount of weight from the previous year, and my mom voiced her concern. The doctor barely glanced up from the chart. "She's fine," he said, waving it off. *Maybe because I didn't look breakable.*

Because my frame—strong, athletic—didn't match their picture of a girl in danger.

Then, almost as an afterthought, he added the words that would echo for years.

"Big-boned."

That's what he called me. Big-boned. I'll never forget that. NEVER. It felt like a punch in my gut so deep that it hurt in my soul. I was starving myself, disappearing—and still, I was too much.

I was dizzy most days, my thoughts constantly circling around food— what I ate, what I didn't, how long I could go without it. The hunger became sort of a high. A punishment. A secret I carried like a trophy and a curse. For me, control looked like restriction. But for others, it might look different. Disordered eating is rarely about food—it's about pain. About shame. About trying to fill a void or silence a scream inside.

Whether we starve ourselves or binge in secret, obsess over every calorie or lose ourselves in the numbness of overeating… the pattern becomes an addiction. A way to survive. A cry for safety in a world that doesn't always feel safe.

No matter the form it takes, it deserves compassion. You are not weak. You are not alone. You are not beyond healing. It's okay if you've used food—or control, or perfection—just to make it through the day.

None of it makes you broken.

This is hard work.

But *you* are worthy of doing it.
Worthy of softness.
Worthy of freedom.
Worthy of love—exactly as you are, even in the unraveling.

I'd scribble in my journal late at night, pages filled with rules and shame:

You ate too much today. Tomorrow, you don't eat until noon. No carbs. No excuses. If you mess up, you're weak. Start over. Do better.

It wasn't about being thin. It was about proving to myself that I was enough—that I had control over *something*.

I didn't know how to explain the emptiness—how I could feel so heavy and so hollow at the same time. On the outside, I looked like a happy teenager—cheerleader, popular, loving family, good grades, always smiling, and lots of friends.

But inside, I was quietly unraveling. Hoping someone would see past the smile. That anyone could help free me from this every minute of torture that I was putting myself through.

Growing up in my generation, girls were thin, and the media praised body types like Claudia Schiffer and Elle Macpherson. I longed to look like them—tall, lean, delicate.

But no matter what I did, that was never going to be me. I had an athletic build. Strong and compact, more like the gymnast Mary Lou Retton—ironically, one of my childhood idols.

But our culture didn't praise athletic girls. The covers of magazines weren't filled with strong legs and muscular backs—they were draped in the ultra-thin, almost sickly images of what we were told womanhood should look like. There was no celebration of curves or power. No message that said we could be strong and still soft, that we could carry both grit and grace. The world didn't teach girls that strength was beautiful—or that we could be bold and beloved all at once.

And I—I was caught in the perfect storm.

Not because I wanted to disappear…

But because I was trying so hard to belong.

If you're nodding along right now, if you've ever felt too much or not enough at the same time—I want you to know, I see you. We didn't fail. Culture did. But we're rewriting that now. Together.

But even with knowing that now, back then, I couldn't see it. I hated my body. My back was wider than most girls', and I had powerful legs. I wanted to shrink.

Looking back, I want to wrap my arms around that younger version of me and tell her how amazing she truly was. It makes me incredibly sad to think about how society shapes young girls—how it tells them, from such a young age, that they must look a certain way to be loved or seen.

And it starts early. Research shows that by age 13, over half of American girls are already unhappy with their bodies. By 17, that number climbs to nearly 80%.

I was one of them. Not just unhappy—but unraveling. And no one knew.

If you're a young girl reading this, or even if the girl in you is still healing, hear me: **You are amazing**. There is only one you. And your gifts, your spark, your story—they matter. Be kind to yourself. You are enough exactly as you are. I promise.

The Darkness I Couldn't Name

I started gymnastics at 3 years old and stayed in it for over a decade. It *was my sport*. It gave me structure, discipline, drive—and a circle of girls I deeply connected with.

But I was always the "bigger" girl on the team. Not fat—I hate that word—but not rail-thin either. Still, I loved gymnastics. It gave me a home. A purpose. Eventually, as my body grew and changed, I drifted from the sport, like many girls do in middle school. But the lessons it gave me stayed.

Then, I started to feel something heavier that I couldn't explain. A fog. A sadness. Depression, though I didn't have a name for it yet. And what confused me most was I couldn't find a reason. What made it worse was the shame — how could I feel this way when my life looked so good? It didn't make sense, and that confusion only deepened the darkness.

On the outside, everything looked fine—better than fine. But on the inside, I was drowning. And that made me feel even more broken. What right did I have to feel this way? I didn't understand it then, but now I know—that's exactly how trauma hides. It burrows in the silence, in the in-between spaces, and convinces you it's all your fault.

In high school, the obsession with being smaller took over. I thought if I could just be thinner, I'd finally be happy. I started controlling what I ate—then restricting, then documenting every single bite. The less I ate, the more in control I felt. It became a game. A high. A terrifying addiction.

I wrote dark, harsh thoughts in my journals. Berating myself. Urging myself to go longer without eating. I was constantly hungry, constantly thinking about food—what I was eating, what I wasn't, how long I could go before I felt weak, dizzy, or passed out.

People around me didn't know. I always showed up looking put together. But inside, I was falling apart. Some even praised how good I looked. Not my family, though. I remember my mom once begging me to eat. "Tara, you have to eat," she pleaded. But I didn't know how. I was lost inside a storm I didn't understand.

My thoughts became so dark they started to scare even me. It was like this heavy, black cloud hovered over everything—following me from room to room, moment to moment. I couldn't outrun it. I couldn't outthink it. It was just there… thick, suffocating, relentless.

My journal entries from that time looked like something out of a horror movie—pages scribbled so hard the pen nearly tore through, angry black ink crossing out entire thoughts, words written over words until they were unreadable. It looked like a war zone. Like a girl fighting to understand herself in the only place she could scream. I'd rip pages out in frustration. Curse myself. Beg the pain to stop. And the worst part? I didn't even know what I was trying to escape.

There were days I didn't want to be here anymore. Not because I didn't love my life or my family, but because the weight of living like this, with this pain, felt impossible to carry. The battle in my own mind was exhausting.

Every minute felt like a fight with myself. And some days, I thought maybe it would be easier if I just… disappeared. That's a hard thing to admit. Even now, typing the words makes my hands shake. But it was true.

And the worst part? I didn't understand *why* I felt that way. Why was I like this? Why was this so hard? Why did I treat myself with such cruelty—with words I'd never say to another soul?

I wasn't that way with anyone else. I loved people. I saw them. I connected with them, no matter their age or story. I've always had that gift—the ability to see someone's heart before they even spoke. I led with empathy, with compassion. I was the first to encourage, the first to wrap someone in comfort. But when it came to me?

I couldn't find an ounce of that same tenderness.

It felt like something was broken inside me. And worse—like I was the only one who couldn't figure out how to fix it. I hated that about myself. I hated my body. I hated how trapped I felt in my own skin. And I hated that no one could see it.

When You Can't See the Wound

There came a moment when I could no longer hide how much I was hurting. I asked for help.

Not because anyone made me, but because something inside me whispered: *You can't keep going like this.*

I agreed to be hospitalized for a week in a facility for girls with eating disorders, depression, and trauma. But once I arrived, I wasn't sure I belonged. Why was I here? Why couldn't I just be okay?

We were behind locked, secure doors. I wore oversized sweats and tried to stay invisible. I listened quietly as the other girls shared stories filled with pain—abuse, neglect, terror. Stories that made my stomach turn. And I sat there, staring at the ceiling, wondering why I was there when I hadn't lived through anything like that.

But at the same time… something about it felt familiar.

I didn't understand it then, but a part of me felt like I *did* belong—even if I couldn't explain why. That confused me more than anything. How could I feel both out of place and exactly where I needed to be?

I remember the group therapy sessions, the conversations between girls who had been through hell and somehow survived it. We weren't allowed razors or anything sharp in our rooms. The doors locked behind us. I listened in horror as they spoke, and I had nothing to add. No tragic backstory. No words. Just this unrelenting ache I didn't know how to name.

I became close with the other girls quickly. That was always me—connecting, hearting, holding space. I saw their pain before I even had the language for my own. And somehow, it grounded me.

Our backgrounds were vastly different. Some had no families. Others had grown up in poverty or neglect. If we'd met outside the hospital walls, the world might have separated us.

But inside, none of that mattered. We didn't know how to name our pain. But we could feel it in each other. They felt like family, even though I wasn't there for long.

I still remember watching them—barely there in their bodies. And me? I was too solid. Too strong. The staff never said it, but I could feel it in their glances. Like I was occupying a bed meant for someone sicker. And maybe they were right. Maybe I wasn't sick enough. But what no one could see was how sick I felt inside—how loud the noise was in my own head. How desperate I was to shrink, to disappear, to quiet it all.

I didn't know then that trauma could live in the body like that. That hunger wasn't just physical—it was emotional. I didn't want food. I wanted peace.

My parents would come visit, and I could feel how much they hated seeing me there. They didn't understand why I couldn't feel comfortable at home or at school. But strangely, in that locked facility, I found something close to silence—a pause from the pain I was trying so hard to outrun. I hated that I needed help. I hated that I didn't know why I was there in the first place. And most of all, I hated that I still couldn't name what was breaking me.

I wish I could tell you that week changed everything. That I left the hospital whole. But healing doesn't happen in seven days. What it did give me, though, was a pause. A brief exhale in the middle of the storm. It didn't fix the pain, but it showed me I wasn't completely alone in it.

I left that hospital still unsure of what had landed me there. I hadn't been abused. I hadn't lived through some horror story.

Or so I thought.

Sometimes, the first crack in the wall we build around ourselves—the one that lets light in—doesn't come with answers. It comes with presence. With knowing someone sees you. And sometimes, that's enough to keep going.

I returned to school, to life, to routine—still carrying the darkness, still trying to outrun something I couldn't name. Thriving on the outside, but a sense of slowly dying on the inside.

While all of that was happening—the obsession with control, the food rituals, the constant self-surveillance—another silence was growing. All the girls around me seemed to be discovering boys, crushes, flirting, first kisses. They whispered in the hallways and wrote names in notebooks, mapping out futures I couldn't even see. But I felt nothing. I wasn't curious. I wasn't interested. I was in survival mode. How could I even begin to let someone in when I barely had a grip on myself?

It made me feel broken in another way—like I was missing some vital part of growing up that everyone else just "had." Like I had been skipped over in the line for normal teenage feelings. I didn't want a boyfriend. I just wanted to feel safe inside my own skin.

After that, my body became a battleground of extremes. I was once the smallest I had ever been—thinner than anyone had seen me—and yet I felt completely numb. I had reached the size I thought would bring happiness, but it never came. It was like I was silently screaming, hoping someone would notice. Someone would see I wasn't okay.

But I was surrounded by love. I had the most caring family. I wasn't neglected or abandoned. That made it even harder—I didn't understand why I felt so lost.

Just as quickly as I had disappeared into thinness, I began gaining weight. By the time I was nearing high school graduation, I was the heaviest I had ever been.

In trying to recover, I started binge eating. My body didn't feel like mine anymore—it felt like punishment. The pendulum swing was brutal.

But still… if you looked at photos of me, you'd never know. I wore the pain well. I smiled. I kept going. I just wanted to feel normal.

It would take more than a decade before the memories surfaced.
Before the truth rose from where I had buried it. Before I understood why the pain had always felt so deep. And when it came, it changed everything.

Now, I understand:
You don't need visible scars or tragic headlines to be hurting.
And just because your life looks good on the outside doesn't mean it feels safe on the inside.

I didn't know then that trauma isn't always loud. Sometimes, it lives quietly in the spaces between what we say and what we feel.

My trauma was invisible. But it was real. And it shaped everything that came after.

Healing doesn't always roar. Sometimes, it begins in whispers—in the quiet courage to tell the truth. And that's where my story begins.

♡ From My Heart to Yours

If you've ever looked in the mirror and wished you were someone else—I see you.

If you've ever tried to disappear while secretly hoping someone would notice—I understand.

Maybe you've lived with the ache of never feeling "enough."

Maybe you've measured your worth by numbers, or silence, or the way others saw you.

Maybe you learned to smile while carrying a weight no one else could see.

I wrote this chapter not just to share what I went through, but to remind you that healing begins when we stop hiding. That your pain doesn't need to be loud to be real. And that you, just as you are, are worthy of love, belonging, and peace.

You are not alone in this.
You are not broken.
You are becoming.

If the little girl inside you is still hurting, still trying to prove her worth—wrap your arms around her today. Tell her she is already enough.

Because she is.

And so are you.

CHAPTER 2

The Pieces That Didn't Fit

"The truth will set you free. But first, it will shatter everything you thought you knew."
–Unknown

The Shifting Foundation

There are some truths we carry for decades without knowing. They live in the body, in the breath, in the silence between smiles. They rise in panic attacks we can't explain. They echo in our journals. They slip into the spaces between who we are and who we pretend to be.

And then, one day, a voice… a memory… a moment—pulls the thread. This was that moment for me.

I'm letting you in on the deepest break in my foundation—the one I didn't know existed until everything I believed about my past came crashing down. The pieces never fit before. But once the truth came forward, I could finally see why. And I could never unsee it again.

This was the hardest chapter to write because it's where the image of my "normal" childhood cracked wide open. It's where the puzzle pieces I couldn't explain finally found their place, and the weight I'd been carrying for so long came into focus.

For a long time, I believed I had a perfect childhood. And in most ways, I did. I loved my family deeply. My parents, siblings, cousins, aunts, uncles, and grandparents were my foundation. Family dinners, holidays, birthdays, and church formed the structure of my life. I was rooted in tradition, love, and loyalty.

But underneath the surface of all that goodness, something was off. A shadow I couldn't name. I lived with a low hum of unease, like something forgotten but not gone. There were feelings I couldn't explain—deep sadness, anxiety, and a heaviness I carried into every room. But I brushed it off. That's what strong girls do.

What I didn't realize then was that I was living with something buried.

I went to college three hours from home—far enough to breathe, close enough to feel safe. I found joy again—joy that wasn't forced or fragile, but real, earned, and rising from somewhere deep within me.

I met some great friends during that time—women I'm still close with today, who brought light and laughter when I needed it most. I changed my major from Business to Exercise Physiology and Movement Science, and suddenly, something clicked. It wasn't just a change in curriculum—it was a coming home to my body, to movement, to strength on my own terms. I began lifting weights consistently, nourishing myself more intentionally, and feeling strength return to my body in a way that wasn't about image—it was about power.

I wasn't fully free from the grip of my eating disorder, but I was inching forward. Then I found bodybuilding, and I fell in love. With the precision. The focus. The solitude and fire of the weight room. There, I felt powerful. There, I felt like I could shape my story, even if I didn't know all the chapters yet. It gave me something to hold onto. For the first time in a long time, I felt steady. Maybe even whole. Life, at last, felt like it was moving forward.

📞 Then Came the Call

It was late afternoon. I remember the light in my college apartment shifting, golden and quiet, the way it does when the sun starts to dip. I was getting ready to go to the gym—something ordinary. Something safe. When I answered the phone and heard my mother's voice, I knew something was wrong. Not by what she said at first, but by how she said it. Her voice was low, careful, like it was moving through molasses.

She told me my younger brother was going to the police to report years of sexual abuse. As she spoke, her words blurred, growing faint, as if she were drifting farther and farther away from me. And then it hit me—an electric shock of memory that stole my breath.

I couldn't hear her anymore. All I could feel were flashes—scenes from when I was 10 years old, buried memories surfacing like a tidal wave.

"Mom," I interrupted, "I know."

She was stunned. "You do? Did you talk to your brother?"

"No," I said. "I know because it happened to me too."

The silence that followed wasn't empty. It was filled with everything we'd never said. And the quiet in my mother's voice stung—it was the sound of a heart breaking under the weight of something unspeakable.

Then I asked, "Did you talk to Sa?"

"No... *whyyyyyy?*"

I could hear the heightened and scared tone in her voice.

"It happened to her, too."

Silence.

That was the moment everything changed.

All the signs—the eating disorders, the anxiety, the darkness I couldn't explain—they suddenly made sense. I had repressed the abuse I had experienced at the hands of a teenage boy we had trusted from church. We all had. I had protected it so well, even from myself. But that protection cost me almost a lifetime—decades of anxiety, depression, perfectionism, and pain I couldn't trace back until the truth surfaced.

Later, I would even come to understand why I'd felt so out of place as a teenager. Why, when my friends were falling in love and navigating first crushes, did I feel nothing? I wasn't broken. I was just protecting the part of me that already knew too much.

And sadly, I'm not alone.

According to the CDC and National Children's Alliance, **one in four girls and one in thirteen boys in the U.S. are estimated to experience**

child sexual abuse, and many are under the age of 12 when it begins. These numbers are heartbreaking, and they only reflect the cases we know about. The truth is, so many carry their stories in silence.

Even more devastating? In roughly **93% of cases**, the child knows the abuser—often someone in a position of trust. A coach. A family friend. A relative. A leader from church. That betrayal runs deep.

I was one of them. For years, I carried the story alone, buried beneath achievement, perfectionism, and a desperate need to feel safe in a world that no longer was. The truth didn't come easily, but once it surfaced, it began to unravel everything I thought I had tucked away.

Like so many others, I tried to silence it. To outrun it. To explain away the anxiety, the eating disorders, the shame. But the body remembers. And eventually, so does the mind.

That silence? It has a cost. And I knew it intimately.

Maybe you do, too. Maybe you're carrying something no one else can see. Perhaps you're battling in silence, and from the outside, no one knows. You look strong. Put together. But inside, you're unraveling.

That was me. For years.

So when the truth finally surfaced, it shattered the image I had built to survive. But it also gave me something I never expected—a chance to stop pretending and start healing.

We don't talk about it enough—how many of us live with trauma trapped in our bodies? Trauma that reshapes how we see the world, how we trust, how we breathe.

Speaking—even when it shakes—is where healing begins.

The trauma cracked my loving family open. There was a silence that settled over us at first, a stunned kind of grief that stretched across phone calls, holidays, and the ordinary moments in between. We were all trying to hold it together, but no one knew quite how to do that. We didn't have a map for this kind of pain—the kind that redefines who you are and how you trust.

We went to court, now ten years after the actual abuse. It was awful and surreal. Our abuser was convicted and went to prison. But the healing? That would take decades.

Justice on paper doesn't always bring peace to the heart. The trial process was brutal in its own way—reliving memories we had fought so hard to forget, seeing them reduced to testimony and timelines. Putting my entire family in the spotlight and under a microscope of horror. And afterward, when the door of the courtroom closed behind us, the world kept spinning... but we didn't. Not right away.

Each of us grieved differently. Some withdrew. Some got louder. Some pushed forward like nothing had happened. But underneath it all, we were all carrying our own version of the ache. We were all now living with some form of **post-traumatic stress disorder (PTSD)**.

None of us had language for it yet, but it showed up—in our bodies, in our silences, in the way we braced for things that hadn't even happened yet.

PTSD is what can happen when the body and brain don't fully recover after trauma. It's more than anxiety. It's more than memory. It's your nervous system trying to keep you safe in a world that once felt dangerous. You're not overreacting. You're reacting to what once felt like a threat to survival.

According to the National Center for PTSD, **about one in thirteen people in the U.S.** will experience PTSD at some point in their lives. And for those who've survived childhood trauma, the chances are even higher.

But numbers don't capture what it's like to live it. The racing heart at a sudden sound. The exhaustion of always scanning for danger. The moments when a memory sneaks in and you lose your breath in the middle of something as ordinary as folding laundry or catching a certain smell.

Family gatherings felt different at first, even when we didn't speak of it. There was love, still—but it was now woven with something else: sorrow, caution, a quiet understanding that things had changed.

And yet... that love remained our anchor. The bond we shared would be tested in ways we never expected. But underneath the ache, something deeper held us. It wasn't perfect. But it was real. And it carried us, even when we didn't have the words yet. Healing didn't happen all at once. It came slowly, in small moments—in honest conversations, in therapy for some, in learning how to say what once felt unspeakable, in recognizing that none of it was our fault.

It wasn't pretty. It wasn't perfect. We withdrew. We lashed out. We got angry. There were slammed doors and heavy silences. Grief doesn't move gently; it stirs up everything buried. Sometimes it fractures you further before it begins to heal.

But we kept showing up. And in the showing up—in the chaos, in the tension, in the love that never fully let go—we began to build again. Falling apart wasn't the end. It was the threshold. Because sometimes you have to let everything unravel before you understand how strong your threads really are. And even in the mess, there was still something sacred holding us.

The truth had set something in motion, but it didn't come without cost. It cracked our foundation. But cracks, I've learned, are where the light eventually finds its way in.

For me, it came in waves. Some days I felt strong, determined to move forward. Other days, I barely recognized myself. I would find myself crying in the car for no reason, panicking in a crowded room, withdrawing from people I loved without even meaning to.

PTSD didn't just show up in quiet moments. I lived it every minute of every day for years. It was inescapable. It ruled my body, my breath, my thoughts. I fought so hard against it, but most days, it felt like it won. Certain songs would come on the radio, and suddenly I was back in that helpless place.

The sound of footsteps behind me could leave me frozen. Certain sounds sent me spiraling. Crowded rooms left me breathless. Even driving—something so ordinary—became terrifying. My body remembered what my mind had only just begun to understand.

The nightmares came often. Sometimes they were vivid, other times just the lingering feeling of dread that followed me into the day. I felt like I was living inside a cage—trapped by fear, pacing within the bars of memories I couldn't unsee.

Depression crept in like a heavy fog. Trust felt impossible, even with people who had earned it. I questioned my worth, my memory, my strength. The need to control everything in my life wasn't about perfection—it was about safety.

What Can't Be Contained

This part of my story—this part of my family's story—is not something that can be neatly told in a few pages.

It's the break that changed everything.
The reason the puzzle pieces never fit before.

Trauma like this doesn't vanish.
It weaves itself into your bones, your breath, your boundaries.
It shows up years later in unexpected ways—in the way you trust, in the way you parent, in the way you flinch when someone raises their voice or steps too close.

I want to be clear—this isn't the whole story.

What happened could fill a book all its own.

But I share it here—in this chapter, in these words, because it shaped everything that came after.

I don't tell it to explain every detail, but to let you in.

To say—if you're holding something heavy, I see you.

Because what we name, we can begin to heal.

And what we share, we no longer bear alone.

A Glimpse in the Mirror

Before I could name what healing might look like, I had to face what the trauma had done—not just to my trust, but to the way I saw myself. It didn't just live in flashbacks or nightmares. It lived in my reflection. It showed up in how I fed myself. How I moved my body. How I avoided my own gaze. Even when the memories stayed buried, the shame found its way to the surface. And so much of it lived in the mirror. There were days I couldn't even look at myself.

Not just because I didn't like what I saw—but because I couldn't even recognize her. Some days, I hated the girl in the mirror. Other days, I just felt numb. Like she was a stranger I was forced to live with.

Maybe you've felt that too.

Maybe there have been mornings when you brushed your teeth with your eyes down, too afraid to meet your own gaze. Or maybe you've tilted your head just so, hoping the angle might hide the parts of you the world never saw beauty in.

We don't talk about it enough—how many women carry this quiet ache. Not just in our bodies, but in how we *see* them.

So if you've ever stood there, wondering why it hurts to be looked at—

Even by yourself—

I want you to know that pain has a name.

And it deserves compassion, not criticism.

You don't have to love your reflection yet.
But maybe, just maybe, you can start by softening your gaze.

What I Thought I Saw

Around that time, I remember standing in front of the mirror one day, staring hard, trying to *see* what everyone else seemed to see.

But I couldn't connect to her—the girl in the glass.
Her eyes looked haunted. Her body was foreign.
Like someone had swapped me out and left a ghost behind.

I reached down and pinched my side, convinced I was grabbing fat. Convinced the curve of my waist was wrong. My hand closed around… nothing.

Just air. How could that be? The image in my mind didn't match the reflection in the mirror—or the reality beneath my fingers.

It was disorienting. Like standing in front of myself and still not being able to see *me*.

That's how distorted our minds can become. The mirror doesn't always reflect truth. Sometimes, it reflects trauma. The kind that lingers in the muscles, in the breath, in the spaces we criticize without question. The kind that rewrites what we see, until even beauty looks like a burden.

I wish I could go back and whisper to her:
You are not too much.
You are not too big.
You are not broken.
You are just… hurting.

But back then, I didn't know the mirror could lie.

The Silence After the Amen

I used to pray every day. I believed the world had goodness, that prayers had power, that faith meant safety. But when the abuse surfaced, something cracked. I stopped praying. I stopped believing. I couldn't understand how a God I'd been raised to trust could allow something so horrific—and from someone within our church. Someone we trusted. Someone *my parents* trusted with their children.

It didn't just shatter my faith—it ripped the foundation out from under me. The very foundation on which my family had built our lives. Church, community, faith—it had all been part of our rhythm, our values, our compass. And now, it felt like a lie.

I walked around carrying that loss in silence. Not just the trauma, but the confusion of no longer knowing what I believed.

I often look at my sons now—11 and 9 years old—and I feel a fierce, aching love. They are loud and wild and full of wonder. They trust the world. They trust me. And that trust cuts me open in the best and hardest ways. I imagine what it would be like for someone to hurt them, and my heart shatters into pieces I didn't know I still held.

That perspective has deepened my healing. It's made the pain personal in a new way, because now I'm not just healing for me. I'm healing for them. For the kind of mother I want to be. For the kind of home I want them to grow up in. I'm more committed than ever to breaking cycles and speaking truth—not just for my past, but for their future.

To my parents and siblings: we didn't choose this, but we survived it. Our foundation cracked, but it did not collapse. And we're still here. Together. Forever.

To the reader: if something inside you is aching, if something from the past is clawing its way to the surface, I want you to know—you are not broken. You are brave. And the weight you're carrying? You don't have to carry it alone.

The Passenger I Didn't Choose

I thought the worst was over once I named it. Once the memories surfaced. Once I finally said it out loud. But trauma doesn't work that way. It doesn't vanish just because it's been spoken. It lingers. It leaks. It finds new places to live—sometimes in ways that make no sense at all.

For me, it showed up behind the wheel. There was a stretch of time in my twenties and thirties when driving became terrifying. Highways felt like battlegrounds. I'd avoid on-ramps at all costs, rerouting entire trips just to keep myself on side roads.

Even when I did make it onto the highway, I had to crack the windows open—just to feel something real, something grounding. I needed air on my skin to remind me I was okay. That I was still here.

TORN HEART

It seems almost silly to share this. That something as simple as driving—something so many do without a second thought—became impossible for me. But it did. I missed out on events, skipped seeing friends, stayed home when I desperately wanted to go—all because I couldn't get there without the constant fear of something happening to me. It is one of the most awful feelings: to feel trapped inside your own body like that—to want to go, but not be able to trust the vessel you're in to get you there safely.

As soon as I neared a ramp, the spiral would begin. Heart pounding. Hands locked on the steering wheel. Breath tightening. A terrifying sense that I might pass out at any moment. It didn't matter that I'd made it through worse. My body didn't feel safe—and it responded like I was in danger. It was awful. I hated it. I hated how powerless it made me feel. How invisible it all was to everyone else. I had always prided myself on strength. But here I was—brought to my knees by a stretch of pavement.

Maybe you've known a different version of this. Maybe you've had your own invisible battles—places or moments that look ordinary to the world but feel like mountains to climb inside your body.

And now? When I drive and see someone hesitate to merge or slow down unexpectedly, I offer them grace. Because maybe they're like I was—just trying to make it through the day without falling apart. And that, too, is strength.

♡ From My Heart to Yours

If you've ever felt trapped in your own skin... if certain sounds, places, or memories make your chest tighten... if you've ever questioned your worth because of what was done to you—know this: you are not alone.

There were years when I lived minute to minute, breath to breath, just trying to make it to the next day. If you're in that place right now, please hear me—you are not weak. You are surviving something that once tried to silence you. And even in the dark, that is powerful.

You don't have to have it all figured out. You just have to keep going.

Even if all you can do today is breathe.

The weight you carry may not be visible. But it matters.

And you don't have to carry it alone.

CHAPTER 3

Muscle, Motherhood, and the Pro Dream

"I am not afraid of storms, for I am learning how to sail my ship."
–Louisa May Alcott

The First Time I Felt Strong

Long before the memories surfaced, my body already knew. I didn't understand it then, but at 16, the weight room became my refuge. I thought I was just learning to lift; in truth, I was lifting more than weights. I was carrying what I couldn't yet name.

My dad was the one who first introduced me to weights. He brought me to the local YMCA because he could see I was fighting my body, and this was his way of helping. He was a strong-willed, competitive athlete himself, so it makes sense that this was where we connected. He may not even recall opening that door for me—but I always will.

I remember walking past the smell of chlorine wafting from the pool area, stepping into the women's locker room with my cassette Walkman in hand—my own music in my ears, my own quiet world forming. That detail alone dates me, I know. But what stands out the most are the feelings: the rubber floors beneath my sneakers, the clang of metal echoing through the space, the intimidating energy of being one of the only girls there.

Now, as a grown woman, I understand how nerve-racking that can be for so many of us—walking into a space where we feel like we don't belong. But back then, I didn't have those words. All I knew was that when I picked up a weight, something inside me shifted.

There were mirrors everywhere, which made me uncomfortable. That might sound strange coming from someone who spent her entire childhood perfecting routines in gymnastics and ballet— sports built on precision, performance, and presence.

I used to love being in the spotlight, sticking a landing, and hearing the applause. Back then, the mirror was just a tool. It helped me get sharper, better, more aligned.

But not now. Not when I was trying to shrink. Not when I was disappearing piece by piece.

On the outside, I was still that outgoing, funny, talkative girl—warm, loving, always playing the part. But inside, I felt like a shadow of myself. A girl moving through fog, just hoping that strength might anchor her before she disappeared completely.

Now, the mirror felt different. It reflected a version of me I didn't understand—one I was trying to hide from, not celebrate. I didn't want to be seen. I didn't want to examine every angle, every curve, every place

I felt I wasn't enough. The spotlight that once thrilled me now felt like exposure.

So I kept my eyes down. Focused on the weights. On the motion. On the burn in my muscles that reminded me I was still here, still trying.

Lifting gave me a reason to eat, to rest, to care about a body I had spent years trying to ignore. It was grounding. Liberating. For someone who had spent so much time trying to disconnect from my body, finally feeling it—really feeling it—was everything.

I don't remember what I lifted or how many reps I did that day. But I remember how it felt. Those first few weeks, I noticed something I hadn't felt in a long time: I could feel my body. Not just see it or criticize it—but *feel* it. And for someone who had spent years trying to disconnect from it, that was liberating. It grounded me. It made me feel safe. It gave me purpose.

The Sport That Held Me

Ten years later, when I met Jack—the man who later would become my husband—there was an unspoken understanding between us: exercise and training weren't just habits. They were part of who we were.

I didn't have to explain why early mornings at the gym helped me breathe easier, or why structure gave me a sense of control. He just got it. There was a mutual respect in knowing we both valued what movement could do for the mind as much as the body.

Years later, it has become something we model—not by preaching, but by living it. Our boys see us move. They see us care for ourselves. They're growing up knowing that taking care of their bodies is a gift, and that strength isn't just about muscles; it's about how you show up for yourself, every day.

Heading into young adulthood, fitness wasn't just a habit—it was a lifeline. I had learned how to channel control in a healthier way, and lifting weights became part of my identity. It grounded me when nothing else did. In my 20s, I started competing in bodybuilding and fitness shows and quickly realized how much I loved it.

That lifestyle was an anchor. It gave me discipline, purpose, and community. My years of navigating an eating disorder made me hyperaware of my body, but in the sport, that focus felt productive. Eventually, though, that fine line blurred, and the obsession came back stronger than before. (That's another story—maybe even another book.)

Even as I navigated depression and PTSD, I kept showing up. The gym was my constant. The stage gave me confidence. The sport gave me purpose. I continued to compete through my twenties and thirties and felt more at home in that sport than I ever had with anything else. Even when I became a mother, I never stopped training. Even through pregnancies, lifting wasn't optional—as long as it was safe, of course.

Despite the mental health battles I was fighting behind the scenes—PTSD, anxiety, depression, trauma recovery—I loved being on stage. Oddly enough, I felt more comfortable in front of a crowd than I did in day-to-day life. The discipline kept me grounded, and the process gave me something to pour my intensity into. I often placed at the top of my class at shows and proudly brought home trophies from every competition I entered. It wasn't about vanity. It was about visibility. For me, it was about being seen.

On the outside, I was thriving—running a busy company, raising two boys, training for fitness competitions. My calendar was color-coded and time-stamped, my meals prepped, my workouts timed to the minute. I was also managing our household—involved in my boys' sports because I loved being on the sidelines, making space for family dinners, birthday celebrations, and all the small in-between moments that stitched our lives together.

I was operating at 110%, but it never felt like enough. Not because I was broken, but because I believed being tired was just the cost of doing it all.

> Studies show that high-performing women—especially those juggling careers, caregiving, and self-expectation—are disproportionately affected by hidden burnout. According to a 2022 Deloitte study, nearly **53% of women** reported feeling burned out, yet many continue to overperform despite internal exhaustion. And in competitive sports, women are **twice as likely** to experience body image-related distress compared to men (NEDA).

I didn't know it then, but I was living inside that silent storm, excelling on the outside while quietly unraveling inside.

I had learned how to function in high gear—and in some ways, I liked it there. It gave me control. It gave me identity. It gave me a buffer between myself and the things I hadn't yet named.

But there's a cost to living that way. A quiet cost. You start to believe that being tired is just normal. That ache is just ambition. That silence is just strength.

Maybe you know that rhythm too—the endless juggling act. The constant pressure to hold everything together while smiling through it. Maybe you've spent your days running from work to home to workouts, checking off boxes, showing up for everyone else… and wondering why you still feel so tired, so stretched, so unseen.

If that's you—I see you. And I want you to know: just because you're carrying it well doesn't mean it's not heavy.

Becoming a Mother, Becoming Whole

Pregnancy was the first time I truly began to see my body through a different lens.

It wasn't about shrinking, sculpting, or striving—it was about creating. And even though I was extremely sick during both of my pregnancies, something sacred was happening beneath the discomfort: I was learning how to care for myself in a new way. I had no choice but to slow down. To listen. To trust that my body—the one I had battled for so long—knew exactly what it was doing.

It's one of the only times in a woman's life when society gives us permission to change—to grow, to rest, to soften. And yet, even that grace has limits. The celebration of pregnancy so often turns back into scrutiny. There's pressure to "bounce back," to erase the evidence that we ever carried life. But what if we honored the change instead? What if we understood that strength and softness can coexist?

It's one thing to embrace our changing bodies. It's another to neglect them completely.

Growing life reminded me how vital it was to take care of mine—not for vanity, but for vitality. I wish we talked about that more.

I've always known I wanted to be a mom. That part of me was never uncertain. But what I didn't know was how much motherhood would give back to me. Not just love, not just meaning—but clarity.

And truthfully, something began to shift in me after I became a mom. Watching my boys grow in all their wild, magical individuality started to open something in me. I loved their uniqueness, their energy, and the way they embraced their bodies without shame.

Slowly, I began to see myself through that same loving lens. Not always. Not fully. But enough to spark a new kind of relationship with my body. It wasn't overnight. But it was a beginning.

Their freedom stirred something in me. Their joy, their confidence, their delight in their own skin—it made me want to love mine too.

My boys didn't just make me softer. They made me stronger.

Strength in the Playroom

We had a playroom for the boys filled with LEGOs, stuffed animals, building blocks, and everything joyful in between. It was loud, messy, magical—the heart of our home during those early years. I spent so much time on the floor with them, building towers and collapsing in laughter, surrounded by the chaos of childhood.

When I couldn't get to the gym, which happened often with two little ones, I found ways to move anyway. I'd sneak in bodyweight squats while picking up toys, do lunges across the playroom, or pushups between rounds of superhero battles. Sometimes, I'd carry laundry baskets up the stairs like they were training tools. Other days, I'd just dance with the boys until we were all breathless with joy.

It wasn't about checking a box. It was about honoring my body—even in the beautiful mess of motherhood.

People often think movement requires a gym. But I knew better. I knew that showing up for myself, even in the smallest ways, mattered. Not just for my physical health, but for the example it set. I wanted my boys to grow up seeing a mother who didn't abandon herself. Who didn't need permission to take up space. Who chose strength in every season.

Even in those early years of motherhood—buried in blocks and bedtime stories—I never stepped away from training. The gym was still part of my rhythm, even if the schedule wasn't always predictable. On days I couldn't make it, I found ways to move at home. But make no mistake: the fire to train never dimmed.

It just adapted.

Because I wasn't done. Not by a long shot.

The Year I Almost Had It All

When Maximus and Magnus were four and six, I made a decision: I wasn't done competing. I had been away from the stage for nearly a decade, but the fire hadn't left me.

In 2019, I returned to the competition stage and placed second and third, standing alongside women ten years younger than me and holding my own. That moment reignited something fierce.

This was it. I was going to go for my PRO card—the pinnacle in the sport, the moment when you're officially recognized as a professional athlete. This wasn't a bucket list. It wasn't a comeback tour. This was the goal I had breathed for over fifteen years. Now, at 42, I was going to train like never before while raising a family and running a business.

This wasn't a whim. And it wasn't about ego. It was a calling; something that lived deep in my chest like breath, like heartbeat, like hunger. I needed it. Not for applause, but for something much more sacred: me.

Maybe you've had that kind of fire too—the kind that doesn't shout, but whispers, *You were made for this.*

Going for my PRO card wasn't just about a title. It was about proving something to myself—that I had made it, not just physically, but emotionally. After decades of struggling with body image, shame, disordered eating, anxiety, and depression, standing on that stage in my 40s would be a declaration: You did it. You didn't give up.

I wanted my boys to see it. To see their mom pursue something big. Something hard. Something that demanded everything I had. I wanted to model for them what it looks like to chase something that lights you up—no matter your age, your past, or your pain.

So I committed. I started prepping like it was already mine. I worked with coaches, mapped out nutrition, tracked recovery, and sleep. I visualized everything—from the suit I'd wear to the moment I'd hear my name. I trained with intention, even when I was tired. Even when the business pulled me in ten directions. Even when mom life was demanding.

Then COVID hit. Everything changed—for everyone. But I adapted. Jack and I built a home gym in our basement, and I kept going. No stage? No problem. I knew this goal was bigger than a single show.

Competitive bodybuilding isn't a hobby. It's a full-time commitment. Add in raising two young boys and running a life sciences recruiting business I had built from the ground up—it was nothing short of a juggling act. But I kept showing up. Day after day. Week after week. I trained through exhaustion, through uncertainty, through every unexpected twist that life threw at me.

And I was thriving.

By the end of 2022, I was 45 and in the best shape of my life. I was strong again. Clear. Ready. Focused. Alive. I started reaching out to suit designers and planning my stage look. I picked show dates. I created vision boards with "PRO" written in bold letters at the center. Every rep, every meal, every early morning was building toward something bigger than a trophy.

I believed in it because I believed in me.

It wasn't about vanity. It was about legacy. About becoming the kind of woman my younger self could have looked up to. The kind of woman my boys could watch rise.

Everything was lining up. I felt unstoppable.

I was ready.

But sometimes, just when you feel strongest, life breaks you open…

I had never felt more alive. The strength I carried wasn't just physical—it was earned. Brick by brick, I had rebuilt my body, my confidence, and my belief that I could still chase something big.

The stage was waiting. My boys were watching. My heart was all in. But life has a way of testing us when we least expect it.

Sometimes, just when we're about to rise, everything we've built begins to shake. I thought I was preparing for the biggest moment of my athletic life.

I didn't know I was about to face the biggest fight of my life.

♡ From My Heart to Yours

If you've ever poured yourself into something because it gave you back pieces of yourself—I see you. If you've chased healing through motion, through progress, through pushing your body when your heart was breaking, you know the fire it takes.

This chapter of my life wasn't about chasing perfection. It was about chasing freedom. Lifting became my language when I didn't have words. Competing gave me purpose when everything else felt like survival.

You don't have to stand on a stage to prove your worth. You don't need a title to earn your place. If you're showing up for yourself, especially on the hard days, that is your victory.

Keep going. Not for applause, but for the power of knowing you didn't quit on yourself.

That's what PRO really means to me. And maybe, to you too.

CHAPTER 4

The Day My Body Screamed

"There is a voice that doesn't use words. Listen."
–Rumi

The Warning Signs We Miss

It was early 2023.

I thought I was doing everything right—training with purpose, caring for my body, finding new ways to love others and myself. I had been consistent, committed, grounded in a vision that felt bigger than me.

Even in the quiet struggles I didn't talk about, I believed I was in the best place I'd ever been. But I was wrong. I didn't know it yet, but life was about to break wide open.

I had just returned from a family trip to Florida. We were finally getting back to routine when COVID hit me—hard. And while my body was physically battling the virus, my mind began to spiral. The uncertainty and isolation made everything feel heavier. I felt fragile, mentally and physically, even before my heart showed signs of breaking. I was down for two weeks, foggy, fatigued, barely moving. But then, just as I was coming out of it, I felt something that stopped me in my tracks.

It was the Tuesday after Mother's Day.

I had just finished my nightly book-and-snuggle routine with the boys. They were tucked in their rooms, lights low, the hum of their sound machines wrapping them in quiet. I was in bed, finally still, letting my body soften into the sheets—when suddenly, everything changed.

I felt something I had never felt before.

Not a twinge. Not pressure. But lightning.

A sudden, electric jolt that shot through the left side of my chest like a blade of fire.

Sharp. Immediate. Wrong. I froze.

My body instinctively stopped—like it was trying to process, to protect, to understand what had just happened. I clutched my chest. Was that real? Had I imagined it?

Then it happened again. And again.

Five… maybe ten minutes of intermittent strikes.

Each wave sharper.

Each one slicing deeper.

I couldn't breathe fully. I couldn't move.

My mind raced faster than my pulse.

What is this?

I had known anxiety. I had danced with panic before—the fast breath, the lightheadedness, the spiraling mind. But this wasn't that. This was something deeper. More physical. More primal.

I called for Jack, but my voice didn't even sound like mine. It was thin. Detached. As if I were already floating above the moment, watching myself from a distance.

When he came in and saw my face, something shifted in his.
He sat beside me, and I tried to explain, but the words came out broken.

"I don't know… it's like a bolt. Like electricity in my chest."

I didn't want to go to the hospital.

I didn't want to be dramatic. I didn't want to be wrong.

I wanted it to pass—like a storm cloud that would just blow over.

But my body… My body was saying **go**.

And still—I didn't.

I picked up the phone and called my mom. My voice was shaky, quiet—part fear, part embarrassment. I told her what happened. The lightning pain on the left side of my chest. How it came and went like waves. I could hear the concern in her voice, but also the pause—the hesitation we both carried.

The pain had stopped. I was breathing again. I wasn't sure if it was serious… or if I had overreacted.

We decided to wait. Just watch it. Rest.

I managed to fall asleep that night curled on my side, one hand resting over my heart. Not because I thought it was my heart. *Because I needed comfort.*

The next morning, I woke up still wondering what it had been. I replayed it in my mind, searching for logic. A pinched nerve? A pulled muscle? Something I ate?

My brain never once went to "heart."

Why would it?

I was healthy. I was strong. I was fit.

Heart problems weren't even on my radar.

I had no risk factors. No reason to believe otherwise.

The week went on with the usual busy rhythm of a family with two working parents and two active young boys. School drop-offs. Lunchboxes packed. Work calls between football practices and story time. But the memory of that night never quite left me.

What was that?

I tried to let it go—to file it away like a bad dream.
But it stayed with me.

Then came Friday morning, just days after those terrifying moments in my bed. I was getting my two boys ready for school—they were five and seven at the time.

I was upstairs in their bedrooms, the usual morning chaos unfolding—backpacks half-packed, pajamas scattered across the floor, and of course, they had missed the bus. So I was driving them in.

I bent down to put socks on one of them, while the other was climbing on my back, full of energy and mischief, treating me like his personal jungle gym.

That's when it started.

A strange tingling in my left fingertips.

The sensation crept up my hand, through my wrist, all the way up my arm, and into my shoulder. Then it moved across my jaw and down the left side of my back.

Just as I stood up, it happened.

A deep, terrifying squeeze in my chest.

This wasn't like before. It wasn't stabbing. It wasn't fleeting.

It felt heavier—more insistent, like something dark and ancient had settled into my chest and refused to leave.

This time, the pain didn't just arrive. It gripped me.
It wasn't sharp—it was deep. Like a pressure building from the inside, slow and menacing.

TORN HEART

Like two invisible hands had wrapped themselves around my heart and started squeezing. Not in a burst—but in a slow, relentless crush.

Every breath felt shallow, like my lungs couldn't fully expand.
My heart… it didn't just ache. It felt like it was collapsing in on itself.
Like something vital was folding, failing, gasping beneath the surface.
And still, I moved through the moment. I smiled. I got the boys ready for school.

But inside? I was unraveling.
The fear pulsed beneath my skin like a second heartbeat. I didn't let it show—not yet—but I felt it rising.
This was different.
Something had truly shifted.
And I was petrified.

But I didn't panic.
Not on the outside.
I couldn't.

I kept my cool, got my boys dressed, zipped their backpacks, and loaded the car. I buckled them in their car seats, smiled, nodded, and asked them if they were excited for the day as if nothing had happened.

I drove them to school like nothing was wrong. But something *was* wrong. Deep down, I knew.

They were laughing, goofing off in the backseat, their little legs swinging, their eyes full of light. And there I was—terrified and pretending.
I couldn't let them see me unravel.
I glanced at them in the rearview mirror and kept my smile steady.

Only after I dropped them off did I call my mom.
My voice cracked as I said it:
"I need you to take me to the ER. Something is wrong."

I didn't know it at the time, but my body had been waving red flags for a while.

Looking back now, I can see how much I was holding. Not just the weight racks in the gym, but the mental weight of running a business, managing a household, remembering every birthday, and showing up at every game. I kept going because that's what I knew. That's what women do. We keep going.

Until something makes us stop.

When the Tests Say You're Fine

They took me in right away—young woman, chest pain, post-COVID. That was enough to trigger protocol. I remember the rush of movement at first—the nurse guiding me to a sterile room, the rustle of gowns, the cold press of electrodes being placed on my chest.

The EKG machine beeped steadily beside me, each tone slicing through the air like a relentless clock of uncertainty. Vials of blood were drawn, vitals were taken, and I was hooked up to monitors that watched my heart like it was a suspect.

For a moment, I felt something almost like relief. Someone was finally validating that the symptoms weren't just in my head.

But then the hours passed.

The urgency faded. The glances grew shorter. The air in the room began to shift from alert to indifferent.

And then the doctor walked in.

He wasn't unkind. But his words were clinical, rehearsed. Like he had said them a thousand times before.

"Your tests look fine," he said. "It might be anxiety. Maybe just lingering effects from COVID."

His voice was calm. Dismissive. Certain.

Mine? It was silent.

Because what do you say when your body is screaming… and no one hears it?

What do you do when every alarm inside you is blaring—but the machines say you're fine?

I wanted to believe him. I did. I wanted to walk out and let it all go. But my chest was still tight. My breath was still shallow. The ache had never left.

And yet… they sent me home.

I remember walking out into the parking lot, the fluorescent lights of the hospital behind me, my chest still aching. I passed a packed waiting room—rows of people coughing, slouched in chairs, waiting for answers I didn't get.

As I stepped through the sliding glass doors, a rush of air hit my face. The sunlight felt too bright. The breeze was too sharp. I paused for a moment, letting the warmth of the sun touch my skin, and still, I didn't understand how they had let me go.

Part of me knew something was wrong. My body hadn't stopped speaking—not in whispers, but in full sentences now. The ache was still there, steady and unnerving. But the other part of me—the part that believes in systems, in protocol, in experts—tried to quiet that voice. I had done everything right. I had asked for help. I had surrendered to the process, trusted the machines, the monitors, the masked professionals behind the curtain. Isn't that what we're supposed to do? Raise the flag, get checked, follow the rules?

So why did I still feel this way?

Why did I still feel small?
Shrunken?
Not just physically, but emotionally—like something had folded in on itself.
Like I had walked in carrying fear, and walked out carrying shame.

And maybe, I thought… maybe they didn't know.
Maybe what was happening inside me wasn't in their textbook.
Maybe their tools weren't built for this. For *me*.

Because their data points don't always include women like me—healthy, fit, high-functioning.
But they also don't include the women who aren't.
The ones who don't look the part.

TORN HEART

The ones whose pain is written off because of bias, assumptions, or invisibility.

We're dismissed for different reasons—but the result is the same.
We're left to question ourselves.
To wonder if we imagined it.
To carry the ache home, alone.

We are the data they don't yet know how to hold.

♡ From My Heart to Yours

Have you ever been told you were fine—
when you knew, deep in your bones, that you weren't?

Have you ever walked out of a doctor's office,
still aching, still afraid,
carrying a pain no one else could see… let alone believe?

If so, please hear me:
You are not alone.
And your body is not your enemy.

She is not broken.
She is trying to protect you.
Even when no one else is listening.

Trust her.
She's been whispering the truth all along.
Not to scare you—but to save you.

I know how hard it is to speak up,
when everything around you tries to quiet your voice.

But that feeling you carry—
that ache, that knowing, that quiet alarm—
it's there for a reason.

Breathe.
Create space to listen.
To feel.
To move toward what you need—not what you're told to need.

Don't wait for permission.
Don't wait to be believed.
Be the breath.
Be the movement.
Be the beginning.

You are the knowing.
You are the miracle.
And you are worth listening to.

PART TWO

THE TURNING POINT

The Fracture.
The Scream.
The Breaking Open That Changes Everything.

CHAPTER 5

SCAD – The Unexpected Heart Attack

"You gain strength, courage, and confidence by every experience in which you really stop to look fear in the face."
–Eleanor Roosevelt

The Silence Before the Signal

At home, I tried to push through. But the pain and pressure in my chest didn't fade. My instincts stirred—quietly, steadily—and I kept thinking, *How could this be happening to me? Maybe it'll pass. Maybe I'm overreacting.*

I didn't know yet what it was. I didn't know it was my heart. I didn't know how close I was to the edge. All I knew was that something inside me felt… off. Different. Unfamiliar.

And I started to wonder—*Am I just too sensitive? Too aware? Too in tune?*

I've always been connected to my body, able to sense subtle shifts and changes. But now that awareness felt like a curse. Was I imagining things? Feeling too much? Was I paying attention to symptoms no one else would even notice?

I was scared, but also unsure if I *was allowed* to be scared.

That tension between knowing something is wrong and trying to convince yourself it's not is exhausting. And quietly painful in a way that's hard to explain.

But it was also the beginning of something I didn't expect: a complete unraveling—and the start of a transformation I didn't yet understand.

For the next 48 hours, I did what I always did—I showed up. I made breakfast. Smiled for my boys. Folded laundry with one hand while pressing the other against my heart. We watched cartoons. I took the dogs outside. I tried to convince myself that if I could just get through the day, maybe I'd wake up tomorrow and feel better. I kept telling myself it would pass—that it had to.

But each task felt a little heavier. I moved more slowly. I felt off—not sick, just unsettled. I knew something was wrong. But I continued to live my life and my moments doing what I always do—caring for others, staying in motion, trying to outpace the fear. I kept hoping it would pass.

But that pressure in my heart never went away. It lingered. Quiet but constant.

Maybe you've felt that too—when your body whispers that something is wrong, but no one around you seems to hear it. Or worse, they hear it and brush it off. We're taught to doubt ourselves, to minimize our pain, to keep going until we can't anymore. But our bodies are wise. Our instincts don't lie.

Please, don't wait for permission to listen to yourself.

Saturday night came. I woke up at 1 a.m. with a horrible pain shooting through the upper/mid-side of my back. It took my breath away. I quietly walked downstairs to the kitchen and took some Advil. I also warmed up a heating pad, hoping it might ease the pain enough to get back to sleep.

Our Frenchie, Moose, who usually slept downstairs on his bed, must've sensed something. It was strange for him to follow me like that. He'd *never* done that at night before.

As I was heading back upstairs, he trailed behind me, those wide, worried eyes locked on mine. I let him come. I scooped him up and placed him in bed with me—something I'd never done before. He curled up at the foot of the bed, right between my feet, almost like he was standing guard.

It felt comforting in a way I couldn't explain. Like he knew. Like maybe I did, too, but just didn't want to name it.

Now, of course, he sleeps in my son's bed. Funny how some things change.

So I lay back down. Let the heating pad rest against the ache in my midback—that strange, quiet pain pulsing behind where my heart lived, Moose curled up between my feet.

And eventually, sleep found me—not because the fear was gone, but because I was tired of wrestling with it.

The Moment Everything Changed

Sunday morning felt normal. At least at first.

It was quiet—which, in our house, usually meant *not normal.*
My boys were watching cartoons in the living room. Jack was reading the news. I had just come upstairs after switching the laundry, already a little winded from the stairs, which was odd.

Normally, we'd be rushing out the door—a sports game, an event, the gym, yoga, something on the calendar. But this Sunday was slow. Still. And for once, it felt nice to have nowhere to be.

I walked into the kitchen, catching my breath. I pressed the button on the Nespresso machine and listened as it came to life, that familiar hum promising the perfect cup. The foam on top—my favorite part. It was one of those tiny joys I always looked forward to.

I walked over to the island and set the coffee down.

And then… ***I felt it.***

The pressure in my heart turned into something much sharper—stabbing, excruciating pain that shot through the left side of my chest like a knife. I clutched the counter, my vision blurring, the coffee mug slipping from my hand.

My entire body broke into a sweat, drenched within seconds. Every inch of me was tingling—like a wave of electricity had surged through my skin. The room began to spin. My breath vanished. I could hear my heartbeat pounding in my ears, loud and erratic, like it didn't belong to me. My legs felt weak, like I couldn't even feel them beneath me.

I stumbled, barely able to stay upright, before Jack rushed in and caught me. I thought I was dying—the pain radiating, my body betraying me. Jack helped me into the next room and eased me into a chair, where I collapsed. I could barely speak, barely breathe. And still, I was trying to hold it together. Trying to be strong. Because that's what I always did. Even as the pain pulsed through me, some part of me was still trying to protect everyone else from it.

Jack was anxious—unsure of what to do first. And like so many husbands do, he called my mom. (*Because isn't that what they all do?* Moms always know what to do, right?)

As the panic in the room grew, I told him something was terribly wrong. In that moment, something in him snapped into clarity. I heard his voice cut through the chaos as he called 911—sharp, urgent, against the backdrop of the TV still playing. My boys kept watching cartoons, their little voices rising in confusion, asking what was going on.

I was drenched in sweat, weak, and scared. A police officer who had been nearby and heard the 911 call arrived within minutes. He stood beside me, offering a steady presence until the paramedics came.

Around me, the house began to shift—Jack's voice rising as his worry turned into action. I was slumped in the chair, dazed and disoriented. My mind felt foggy. My body, foreign. It was as if I was hovering just outside of myself—aware, but detached—watching it all from somewhere else.

Then came the sirens. Firetrucks, ambulances, first responders—they surrounded me in waves, their presence a blur of movement and sound. Jack had given the boys a task: keep the dogs behind the gates. It gave them something to do, and for that, I was grateful. They didn't seem scared—just wide-eyed and oddly thrilled about the firetrucks. Their excitement felt like a small mercy.

I glanced down and noticed I was wearing my favorite bright pink pajama set, the one with little hearts all over it, and matching slippers.

The polish on my toes, by some ridiculous twist of fate, matched my pajamas perfectly. For a split second, through the panic, I thought, *Well, if I'm going to die today, at least my toes are done and I look kind of cute.*

It was surreal—being surrounded by first responders, wires and cuffs being placed on my arms and chest, voices checking vitals, hands working quickly. I remember three to five people hovering over me, attaching EKG leads, and taking my blood pressure.

And still, when the monitor came back showing nothing urgent, the concern about my heart seemed to slip from their focus. I was surrounded by care, but not clarity. And that made everything feel even scarier.

They loaded me onto a stretcher—the warm May air brushing against my skin as they wheeled me outside. Everything felt distant, like I was watching it all happen from underwater. I caught a glimpse of my boys on the porch, standing beside my mom, who had just arrived. They were watching everything unfold—a little confused, a little worried, but still playful in their own way, like they knew something was happening but didn't yet understand the weight of it. I gave them a small wave and a smile—just enough to let them know I was okay, or at least trying to be. They smiled back. I felt weak. And confused. Uncertain. I wasn't sure who to trust or what to think, so I let the medics take over.

As the ambulance doors shut, the world felt muffled. I stared at the ceiling, trying to ground myself, trying to understand what was happening. I couldn't help but think of all the people who had been in the back of an ambulance like this—lying here, staring up like me. What were they surviving? What had they lost? It was both a comforting and terrifying thought. To know I wasn't the first. To know I wasn't alone. But also to know how many stories had ended in this same space. I closed my eyes, willing myself to stay calm, to stay present, to stay here.

They drove me back to the same hospital that had released me just 48 hours earlier. I remember the jolt of the wheels as they rolled me out of the back of the ambulance.

I was alert, watching as the ER doors slid open once again. I was back—still in pain, still without answers—but this time, I wasn't walking in. I was being wheeled in, my chest sore and heavy with pressure, not knowing what was waiting for me on the other side.

This time, it felt more serious. A quiet kind of urgency filled the air. Nurses moved quickly, placing leads on my chest, taking blood, and checking vitals. I answered their questions the best I could, still feeling foggy and unsure.

It all happened fast, but I remember catching the difference—their tone was more focused. I wasn't being brushed off this time. That gave me a strange sense of comfort, even though I was still confused about what was actually happening.

Jack sat beside me, quiet, tense. I could see the worry etched across his face. We were both just waiting—hoping for someone to tell us what this was.

The Split Second Before a New Life Begins

Then a doctor came in. Calm, composed—don't they all seem that way? He sat down next to me, looked at me seriously, and said, "Tara, there's a protein in your blood called troponin. It's elevated."

I blinked. "Okay… and?"

He explained gently, "That means there's been damage to your heart. We're sending you to a larger hospital in Boston. You need advanced cardiac care—now."

I half-laughed, not because it was funny, but because it still didn't make sense. I told him I had a yoga class I was planning to go to. This just didn't feel like something that could be real.

But then I looked at Jack. His face had gone pale. And that's when I knew this was happening. This was real.

♡ **From My Heart to Yours**

If you've ever had a gut feeling that something wasn't right and been told it was all in your head, I wrote this chapter for you.

If you've ever doubted your own body because someone else did, if you've been made to feel dramatic, fragile, or dismissed, you are not alone.

This is where everything began to break. But it's also where something stronger began to rise: my voice, my self-trust, my vow to never ignore myself again.

We are taught to be low-maintenance, to push through, to smile through warning signs. But your body? It remembers. It speaks. And it will not stop asking for your attention.

Please don't wait for permission to listen to yourself.
Please don't ignore the knowing you carry inside.

You are not imagining it.
You are not too much.
You are wise. And you are worth fighting for.

CHAPTER 6

The Fight to Be Seen

"Your silence will not protect you."
–Audre Lorde

The Collapse of Control

It had been nine hours since I was first taken out of my house to the local ER, and I was just now arriving in Boston by ambulance. The ride had been quiet, except for the constant beeping of machines. There was an EMT sitting beside me, watching over my vitals as we made the drive.

I don't remember much of what I was thinking, only that I felt stunned. Disconnected from myself. My chest still ached, my thoughts blurred. I wanted to believe I was finally being taken to the right place—a cardiac center. I had so many questions. I was hoping for answers. But instead of being ushered into a room or met with reassurance, they placed me in the hallway.

The bright lights pierced my eyes. Noise was everywhere—nurses moving quickly, machines buzzing, patients moaning in pain. It felt like being thrown into the middle of a battlefield. I had a pounding headache and a rising fear that something was being missed. I clutched my chest, unsure what was happening inside me but certain it wasn't right.

They finally moved me, but only into a triage area. I had no idea I would stay there until the next day—in the middle of chaos, surrounded by suffering. No door to close and no one to reassure me I was going to be okay.

The ER is a place of suffering—confusion, desperation, and noise. I was frightened, confused, and in pain. Doctors, fellows, and nurses came and went, doing routine exams and tests. Despite my symptoms, no one seemed to believe anything was seriously wrong.

The beeping of machines haunted me, and I hadn't had anything to eat or drink for so long. They kept telling me I couldn't until they knew what tests I'd need.

That might make sense to some, but when your body is trained to eat and hydrate like clockwork, the system revolts. My body wasn't just tired, it was alarmed by the sudden shift from precision to deprivation.

All I wanted was a room. Just a small space where they could shut the door, and I could try to relax. But the doors stayed open. The trauma came in and out. I lay there in the noise, the motion, the fluorescent glare—and I only felt worse. When they performed an echocardiogram—which hurt while they pressed against my chest—it revealed abnormalities. Even after everything, I hadn't expected that. Part of me still believed my heart would come back clear.

Soon after, a cardiologist came in and told me I'd needed a cardiac catheterization—a procedure where a thin, flexible tube is threaded through an artery (usually in the wrist or groin) into the heart. A special dye is injected to help them see inside the vessels and chambers, looking for tears, blockages, or anything that doesn't belong. I'd heard of it before. But until I was living it—waiting for it—I didn't understand how critical it was. What it revealed. What it could mean.

Still, I said, "Okay. Let's go." But that didn't happen right away. I waited. And waited. Hour after hour passed. I held onto hope that by nightfall, I'd have answers. But the night came... and I was still in the ER. Still in limbo. Still hooked to wires with no news. Then came the words I didn't want to hear:

"It will happen in the morning."

No. No. No. I was heartbroken. I had built my entire identity on pushing through, but I was unraveling. I had to shift my mindset—fast—or I was going to lose it. Okay, I told myself. Just make it through the night.

But I didn't sleep. The noise, the fear, the sadness of it all pressed in. I was hooked to monitors and blood pressure cuffs, lines running from my arms to moving carts and wall ports. My body ached. My belly protested. Just weeks ago, I had felt on top of the world. Now I felt like I was sinking into the bottom of an ocean.

And still, in that sterile room, something unseen held me. Like the quiet strength of a mountain beside me—unmoving, but somehow enough. I don't know if it was hope, or memory, or something in between. But in the deepest part of that night, I felt carried.

Maybe you've felt that too—the moment when the ground disappears and all you can do is hold on. When something crashes through your world and you're left breathless.

And yet… there's something that stays. A thread, a pulse, a presence. You don't always see it, but you feel it—holding you, even in the dark.

The Fight for Answers

The next morning, I was eager to go to the OR. Funny, isn't it? To be desperate for answers, even if they might hurt. They told me I would go at 10 a.m. But 10 came and went. I kept asking, kept checking. Hour after hour passed. I watched nurses at the station laughing, checking their phones. I was still lying there. Still waiting.

My will to push—the one that's carried me through my life—kicked in. I spoke up. And kept speaking. Until someone finally heard me.

Why do women have to fight to be believed? Why must we raise our voices just to receive basic care?

> Research shows that women are significantly more likely to be dismissed or misdiagnosed in emergency rooms, especially when reporting cardiac symptoms. A study published in the *Journal of the American Heart Association* found that women under 55 were seven times more likely than men to be misdiagnosed and sent home during a heart attack.

Hour after hour, they told me I was next. My heart was aching—not racing, not fluttering, but sore in a way I didn't know a heart could feel.

It burned like an open wound someone was pouring water over. Constant, raw, relentless. It reminded me with every beat that something was wrong. And each hour, I stayed in that bed, hooked to IVs, blood pressure cuffs, monitors that beeped in a steady, soulless rhythm that seemed to mock my helplessness.

At some point, they moved me into a very small ER room—but not alone. Another patient was there, and food was brought to them multiple times. I lay there starving, my stomach twisting at the smell, my head pounding from the deprivation, the fluorescent lights, and the wait that felt endless.

Time started to blur. Minutes felt like hours, and hours passed without meaning. There was a clock on the wall, and I couldn't stop looking at it, as if staring would make it move faster. But it didn't help. It only reminded me how long I'd been lying there, unseen. Everything felt like waiting. Waiting to be helped. Waiting to be believed. Waiting to feel like myself again.

I was exhausted. I missed my boys. I kept thinking about them, wondering if they were scared and how they were processing it all. Jack had been driving back and forth between home and the hospital, taking care of them, trying to be everywhere at once while still showing up for me. It was a complete mess. I felt all of it. I missed my life.

Maybe you've had a moment like that. Where everything you've worked for—every routine, every title, every role you play—just slips through your fingers. And suddenly, you're not sure who you are without it.

I'd had enough. I managed to swing my legs off the bed to the side and shuffle myself off the mattress. Then, I ripped the IV cords from the wall ports they were secured to and shuffled over to the RN station. I was lightheaded, weak, but determined.

"When will I be taken?" I asked.

"Soon," they said. Again.

Tears poured down my face. I didn't have words anymore—just tears. I started to slowly walk toward the exit.

Jack was freaking out, calling my mother, and I remember thinking, "What is she going to do?" I laughed a little in my head, even in that moment. I had completely lost my mind in there, and I didn't think I could make it another minute.

Jack managed to get me back into bed, but not until I demanded more help. Within an hour, I was finally being wheeled into the OR for the cardiac catheterization. I had never been so grateful to be going anywhere in my life.

The Name for the Pain

In the OR, the doctors and nurses moved around me with practiced urgency, each person focused on their part. I was placed on the OR table, and they began to prepare me for the procedure. Large TV screens lined the left side of my body, and I lay there staring up at them, trying not to panic.

Someone gently placed an oxygen mask over my face. The cold plastic against my skin felt both grounding and surreal. As I lay there, exposed under the lights while they were draping my body with blankets, I wondered what they thought when they saw me. My body was young, lean, and muscular—the result of years of disciplined training. I imagined that most patients they saw didn't look like me, and I wondered if it surprised them. Not in a vain way, but in that quiet, painful way we ask ourselves: do they see me and second-guess why I'm here?

I was clearly fit, but still so broken. This was happening. I stared up at the lights, at the ceiling tiles, at the blur of movement around me, trying to make sense of how I'd gotten here. It had been nearly 48 hours since I first felt that stabbing pain.

Still, I had no answers. Just this pressure in my chest, this ache in my heart, and the silent question that had followed me from one hospital room to the next: What if they're wrong?

They explained they'd be threading a small tube through my wrist into my heart. A dye would help them see what was happening inside.

"Tara," one doctor spoke up," we don't think anything is wrong, but we take your symptoms seriously."

I closed my eyes.

Then I heard it—the sentence that would change everything.

"Tara, I'm so glad we did this. We found something."

They found something? WHAT?!?

"Yes," the doctor continued. "There's an artery in your heart that tore. It's called a spontaneous coronary artery dissection—SCAD. You had a rare kind of heart attack."

Heart attack? Me? How? My mind went blank.

The Long Night

SCAD.

A word I had never heard before now lived inside my body. And I didn't know what to do with it. How did this happen? What caused this?

They wheeled me into a post-op recovery space. The OR lights dimmed behind me, but the weight of what I'd just heard hadn't lifted.

The doctors had gone to tell Jack. I imagined his face—how it would fall when he heard the words. I pictured his eyes, searching for understanding, for control, for a way to fix this. And there was nothing I could do from where I lay.

A strange wave of relief settled over me—*something was wrong*. I had known it. I hadn't imagined it. The fight to be seen hadn't been for nothing. But now I had to face this thing I didn't understand. This tear. This invisible rupture in the organ that had carried me through so much.

I was beyond exhausted—physically, emotionally, spiritually. I had been fighting for days just to be believed. And now that the battle had cracked open the truth, I felt too tired to hold it.

Then came the words I never expected:

"There are no cardiac beds available. We may have to send you back to the ER."

No. Please, no.

Tears welled instantly. I could barely breathe as it was, and now they were going to place me back in the chaos I had just escaped?

"I'm not safe there," I whispered. "I can't go back."

I wasn't loud, but I was firm. Clear. Honest.

And someone heard me.

Two nurses stayed with me in that moment—guardian angels in scrubs—refusing to let me disappear back into that fluorescent storm. One of them introduced herself: "I'm Mary."

The second I heard her name, something inside me softened and my eyes filled with tears. Mary was my grandmother's name, and it echoed through my family—my Auntie Maryalice, my other grandmother Marilyn. All three women, now in heaven. In that instant, I knew I was going to be okay. It felt like they had sent her to me.

Both nurses saw my fear, and though their shift had ended long before, they stayed. They refused to let me disappear back into that fluorescent storm. They waited with me until, by some grace, a room finally opened up.

It was nearly 1 a.m. when they finally wheeled me in. The hallway lights blurred into streaks as I stared up from the gurney—tired, grateful, undone.

I closed my eyes and let the darkness wrap me as they brought me into a room on the cardiac floor.

♡ From My Heart to Yours

If you've ever felt something deep in your body—and been told it was nothing—you are not alone. If you've sat in waiting rooms, whispering your truth louder and louder until someone finally listened, I know the weight of that silence.

This wasn't just about a torn artery. It was about the system that almost missed it. It was about the part of me that started to doubt my own knowing, because the world around me didn't believe it.

But I want you to know this:

Your body is wise.
Your instincts are not imaginary.
And your voice is worth raising—even when it shakes.

Sometimes survival means being loud. Sometimes it means walking to the nurses' station with tears streaming down your face. Sometimes it means demanding to be seen, even when you're exhausted from the fight.

You don't need anyone's permission to advocate for yourself. You just need to remember: *You know you best.*

And that knowing? It might just save your life.

CHAPTER 7

The List That Broke Me

"Once you choose hope, anything's possible."
–Christopher Reeve

The Strongest I Had Ever Been

My body had never been stronger. Fitness shows ahead. PRO Card in sight. A thriving business. A beautiful family. The picture of health and wellness. Or at least, that's what I believed, until a doctor looked me in the eyes and said the words that shatter me—something is wrong with your heart.

That was the moment my heart tore open in every possible way.

I didn't know it then, but this was the beginning of becoming the woman I was always meant to be. But first, I had to survive the weeks and months—and years—of physical pain, emotional devastation, and forced surrender.

I spent a week in the hospital, hooked up to machines, pumped full of medications I couldn't pronounce. Everything that had once grounded me—my routine, my movement, my sense of control—vanished. No gym. No meal prep. No yoga mat. No work. No making lunches for the boys. I wasn't in charge of anything anymore. And that terrified me.

The tear was deep, buried in the bottom of my LAD—the left anterior descending artery. Surgery wasn't an option. It was too risky. They told me any attempt to go in could cause more damage than healing. So I had to wait. Let it heal on its own. Trust my body. But how do you trust a body that broke without warning?

I was placed on a cardiac floor, one with thirty other patients—most of them in their 70s, 80s, or 90s. My roommate was 92. I was 46. I felt invisible. Out of place. Like I didn't belong there—and yet, I did.

In my mind, this was temporary. I'd rest, heal, and get back to life. Back to lifting. Back to yoga. Back to my business. Back to everything that made me… me.

But then the doctor came in. A cardiologist. A teaching doctor with nearly four decades of experience, the kind of presence that carried both authority and weariness, surrounded by a crew of trainees, all crowding around my bed. For a split second, I felt like I was in an episode of Grey's Anatomy—but this wasn't television. This was my life, my heart on the line. I was ready. I had scribbled questions on the back of a hospital magazine, writing in messy ink because my vision was blurry from medication, my mind foggy from trauma, and IV tubes tangled across my chest.

I looked up, hopeful.

He handed me a few stapled pages and said…

"Tara, you've had a spontaneous coronary artery dissection—a SCAD. It's rare, and the truth is, we don't know that much about it. In fact, you're probably the 10th case I've seen in forty years. And I've never had a patient as fit or as young as you."

Spontaneous Coronary Artery Dissection (SCAD) is an emergency heart condition that occurs when a tear forms in an artery wall and blocks blood flow to the heart. Unlike a traditional heart attack caused by plaque buildup, SCAD primarily affects women under 50 who often have no prior risk factors for heart disease.

According to the American Heart Association, about 90% of SCAD cases occur in women, many of whom have no prior risk factors. It is one of the leading causes of heart attacks in women under 50, and yet it remains under-researched and often misdiagnosed.

The List That Broke Me

Then I looked at the top page.

"Things You Can Not Do."

The first line: **No weightlifting**.
A sketch of a barbell beside it.
I froze. My eyes burned.

The second: **No hot yoga.**
Tears spilled.

Then: **No high-intensity cardio. No HIIT training.**
Now I couldn't breathe.

And more followed:
No extreme temperatures.
No saunas. No hot tubs.
Even altitude could be dangerous.

WHATTT??????? This is impossible. How could this be?

I choked back sobs and tried to stay upright in the bed. I told myself I could handle this. Surely, it was temporary. So I asked, "How long do I need to avoid these things?"

The doctor looked at me gently.

"Tara... no. You can't do these things anymore. Not ever."

In one sentence, everything I had built—everything that made me feel strong, safe, and alive—was stripped away. I didn't know how to exist without movement. Without challenge. Without strength. And now I had to.

It felt like someone had torn pages out of the book of who I was, and I wasn't sure what was left.

It wasn't just my artery that tore. It was the life I knew, the identity I loved, and the body I thought I could trust.

That sense of self had taken decades to build. It wasn't just about lifting weights or doing yoga—it was how I proved to myself that I was strong, that I could handle anything. My body was my sanctuary, my outlet, my armor. In a world that can make women feel powerless, movement has always been my way of taking power back.

So when they handed me that list, it didn't feel like a restriction. It felt like a dismissal of everything I had fought for—erased in one quiet moment.

Who was I now, if I couldn't do the very things that had once saved me?

Well, I could surely make sense of this if I knew why it happened. What was the cause? Did I do something wrong? I told myself that if I just had the answers, I could 'fix' it moving forward, no matter how long the road. But then came the second blow.

"We don't know much about what truly causes SCAD."

This had to be a joke. The doctor listed off possibilities—stress, hormones, hidden conditions—but none of them felt like facts. The truth was, no one really knew. And in that moment, my world felt smaller than it ever had before.

The Weight of What I Couldn't Hold

The restrictions weren't just about workouts—they reached into every corner of my life. I wasn't even supposed to lift anything over thirty pounds. Did that mean I couldn't scoop up my boys when they ran into my arms? Would I have to tell them they couldn't jump into my lap or be held the way they were used to?

And what about Gemma—my 100-pound bullmastiff who loved to crawl up onto my chest for snuggles? She didn't know about SCAD. She just knew home. Comfort. Me. And now, even that felt uncertain.

I didn't understand what SCAD truly was yet, or how deeply it would affect every corner of my life. All I knew was this: everything had changed, and I was going to have to learn how to live differently—one breath, one decision, one day at a time.

♡ **From My Heart to Yours**

If you've ever felt like your body betrayed you—like the life you knew slipped through your fingers—you're not alone.

If you've had an identity built on strength, only to wake up one day and find that strength stripped away—I know that ache.

If the rules changed overnight, if your body no longer felt like home, if you sat in a hospital bed trying to understand what was left of you—you're not alone.

This wasn't just about losing movement. It was about losing a part of me I had fought to earn. But I'm still here. And so are you.

Keep going. Especially on the days it doesn't make sense. Especially when you feel like you've been erased.

You are rebuilding.

The pieces might come back in a different order, but they're still yours. And when they do, they might just build someone stronger than you ever imagined.

CHAPTER 8

When Recovery Isn't Linear

"Every moment of light and dark is a miracle."
–Walt Whitman

In the Hospital

At first, I didn't know how long I'd be in the hospital. Each morning, I held out hope—maybe today would be the day I could go home. I waited for the cardiologist's rounds like a student waits for test results, listening closely to footsteps in the hallway, willing them to bring good news. But most mornings brought the same quiet words: "Not just yet."

Then came the hardest part—calling my boys to tell them Mamma wasn't coming home that day. Again. I could hear the disappointment in their voices, and it pierced me deeper than any needle ever could. I tried to sound upbeat, to protect them from the truth. But inside, I felt cracked open. Like my heart had broken in more ways than one.

Looking back, I know I needed to stay. I needed monitoring, answers, and rest. But at the time, I was wrapped in fear and disorientation. The days blurred together. I was too tired to move much, yet my mind wouldn't slow down. I didn't feel like myself. I didn't feel like a patient, either. I felt like a stranger inside my own skin—fragile, uncertain, no longer in control.

And under all of that was this restless ache to understand what was happening—*really* happening. I wanted to ask better questions, to understand what SCAD truly meant, what recovery would look like, and how I could protect myself from it happening again.

But I felt trapped inside the chaos of healing, too weary to advocate, too overwhelmed to process. I clung to what I was told, nodded through medical explanations, and tried to stay afloat in a sea of language that felt foreign.

One day, I decided I wanted to take a short walk. Nothing big—just a few steps outside my room. I sat up slowly, letting my feet find the floor. The wires and IV lines shifted with me, a tangle of quiet reminders that I wasn't going far.

I stood carefully and gathered the machines beside me. Reaching the doorway felt like a small milestone. I hadn't seen the hallway in days.

I shuffled forward, holding the IV pole close as I walked down the cool tile floor. And then I saw it—a small sign taped to the wall:

> *"Happiness can be found even in the darkest of times, if one only remembers to turn on the light."*

That quote stopped me in my tracks. Not because it was profound or new, but because it was something. It was light in the tunnel. Hope taped to a wall.

I paused, standing there in my hospital gown, and felt tears well up. That quote didn't take away the fear or the pain, but it reminded me I wasn't entirely lost. It showed me there was still something to hold onto. In a week filled with blood tests, medication charts, and sleepless nights, that small piece of paper was the first thing that made me feel connected to something bigger than my diagnosis. But with the looming question I had: Was I going to make it back to myself?

I didn't know it yet, but parts of my heart had been tearing long before SCAD ever arrived. Quiet tears—emotional, invisible—the kind that go unnoticed until they demand to be felt.

Coming Home

The day I finally came home was a mixed bag of relief and quiet fear. Jack wheeled me through the hospital's double doors, and as we stepped outside, the heat wrapped around me like a sudden wave. The sun hit my face with the force of opening a boiling pot—sharp, blinding, disorienting.

I turned my head, eyes squinting, needing a second to catch my breath. It felt like stepping out of a dark cave into unexpected light—overwhelming in its intensity, almost too much for a body still learning how to be upright again.

I was sore. Slow-moving. Anxious. But I was going home.

Walking into my house was such a relief—a strange kind of homecoming that held both comfort and sorrow. My boys rushed to me, arms flung wide, but with a gentleness they'd never had before. They held me carefully, as if I might break. And maybe, in some ways, I already had.

I sank into the couch, my own soft pillow under my head—familiar, forgiving. Maximus sat near me, gently adjusting it so my head rested on his lap, like it was his job to protect me. Magnus curled up at my feet, not saying a word, just being close. Moose tucked himself along my side, his warm breath steady against me. And Gemma—regal and grounded as ever—lay beside the couch like a quiet guardian. I reached down and brushed my fingers through her fur. She didn't move, but I swear she knew.

They had all missed me. And in that quiet—that rare, heavy silence—I felt the ache in the room. They knew something had happened. They couldn't name it. But their bodies told the story.

And so did mine.

The New Reality

I returned home with a level of exhaustion I'd never known. My heart felt tender and foreign. Sore 24/7, with symptoms and side effects in the recovery that were hard to manage. There were medications lined up on the counter. Blood pressure cuffs and pill organizers I never thought I'd need.

Most nights, I'd wake up drenched in sweat—1 a.m., then 2 a.m., then 3 a.m.—heart pounding, panic crashing over me like a wave. I was terrified to fall asleep. Terrified I wouldn't wake up. I'd lie there in the dark, palm pressed to my chest, feeling the dull, constant soreness under my hand. Was this normal? Was it happening again? My mind would spiral as I checked my pulse, again and again, hoping it wasn't too low, too fast, too slow, too anything.

And in the silence, one question echoed louder than the rest:
Were my boys going to lose their mom?

Some nights, I'd wake Jack up, my voice shaky, my hands clammy, convinced something was wrong. I didn't want to scare him, but I couldn't carry it alone. He never said he was afraid, but I know he was. Seeing *me* scared—that was new. And neither of us really knew what to do.

He'd sit up, unsure of how to help, watching me check my pulse for the tenth time. Sometimes he'd ask if I needed to go to the ER. Sometimes he'd just stay awake beside me, not saying much, but letting me know I wasn't alone.

I missed the hospital in a strange, aching way—not the beeping machines or sterile smells, but the sense that someone was always watching, always ready if something went wrong.

At home, it was just me. Me and this fragile, frightened heart I no longer trusted. And in those moments, I felt more alone than I ever had before.

But the hospital hadn't felt safe, either—not really. I was surrounded by care, yet no one could give me clear answers. I was hooked up to machines, monitored by experts, and still, I was lost in a maze of uncertainty. The security I longed for was never quite real. Not there. Not here. Not anywhere.

The Identity Whiplash

Everyone talks about surviving a heart attack like it's the finish line, but it's not. It's the beginning of a thousand invisible battles. For me, surviving SCAD didn't come with relief. It came with waves of confusion, grief, and fear. I thought I'd feel grateful just to be alive, but some days I didn't. Some days I felt lost. Now I was on a healing journey—one that felt both necessary and never-ending. And not knowing enough about SCAD to help me heal, my mind went off in a hundred directions. The unknowns became their own kind of wound, leaving me grasping for answers that didn't exist.

Just as I began to find my footing, I was met with a new layer of fear: the reality that SCAD could strike again. This wasn't a one-time crisis. It was something I might have to live with forever. The percentages were considered low, but when a doctor tells you there's a 20% chance of it happening again, it doesn't feel low—it feels like a shadow you can't outrun.

> **SCAD** (spontaneous coronary artery dissection) is not a typical heart attack. It's not caused by plaque buildup or clogged arteries. It's a spontaneous tear in the inner lining of a coronary artery—a tear that disrupts blood flow and causes damage.

One of the cardiologists told me, "Tara, your arteries are pristine." And yet, I had a heart attack. That's the terrifying part. It can happen to healthy, active women—and it often does.

Just as I was starting to catch my breath from one wave of fear, another rolled in.

That's when they told me about fibromuscular dysplasia—FMD. A condition that causes abnormal cell growth in the arteries, FMD is found in about half of all SCAD patients.

I was told I needed a full-body CT scan, head-to-pelvis, to rule it out. If I had it, the treatment would be different—more intense, longer recovery, greater risks.

To say I was scared would be an understatement. I had just been through a heart attack. I was barely sleeping. I could still feel the weight of fear sitting on my chest every morning when I woke up. And now, this?

I remember the day I went for the scan.

It was just a couple of weeks after coming home from the hospital. I tied the hospital gown behind my neck, the fabric cold and thin against my skin. The snap at the top of the gown made me flinch. Back then, everything made me flinch.

I waited to be called in, sitting in a stiff chair, surrounded by strangers and fluorescent light. My name was finally called, and I was led into the scanning room—sterile, humming, clinical. I lay down on the table and felt the cool metal beneath me.

As the machine began to hum and move, slowly pulling my body inside, I stared up at the blank ceiling. My mind wasn't quiet.

I thought of all the women everywhere who had lain down on similar tables, wondering the same thing: Is something terribly wrong with me? Will everything change after this?

Tears slid silently down my cheeks and into my ears. I didn't move. I didn't speak. I just let them fall. When the scan was over, I slowly got dressed in silence and walked to my car. I drove home in a daze—mentally drained, emotionally spent, my body still aching from everything it had already been through.

Then came the waiting.

Sometimes the scariest moments aren't the tests themselves, it's the silence afterward. The waiting. The not knowing. If that's where you are right now, hold on. Answers don't always come quickly, but that doesn't mean they won't come.

A couple of days passed. I stayed off social media. I didn't check in with the online SCAD groups I had joined. I couldn't take in anyone else's fear. Not that week. I needed to protect my energy—to stay just above the surface of my own hope.

Finally, my doctor called.

"Good news, Tara. You don't have FMD."

I exhaled for what felt like the first time in days. Relief came in a wave. Okay, Okay. That's one less thing. That's one less shadow.

But even in that moment, I couldn't just feel happy for me because what about the women who don't get this call? What about the ones who survive SCAD, only to be handed another diagnosis, another mountain to climb?

It broke my heart to think of them. To imagine their fear layered with more uncertainty. I couldn't stop wondering: ***How many women have to endure this kind of invisible devastation and are still expected to carry on like nothing happened?***

I was grateful. But I was grieving too. For the ones still searching for answers. For the ones still scared. For the ones who never got to hear, "good news."

That's when I knew—this wasn't just about me anymore.

But for now, I could move forward.

For now, I could focus on finding the right doctors, building a recovery plan, and reclaiming some kind of peace.

But I was still lost. Still unseen. Still waiting for someone to show up and say: "We understand SCAD. We see you. We can help."

I was living in one of the most medically advanced places in the world, and yet, it felt like no one could tell me what to do next.

Still, something inside me held on to belief. There had to be someone. A team. A hospital. A doctor. Someone who would know.

I just had to find them.

The truth is, when your heart breaks, literally or metaphorically, the recovery is rarely a straight path.

There are steps forward and spirals back. I was trying to return to life, to normalcy, but my body didn't feel like mine.

My energy was inconsistent. My thoughts raced. I couldn't sleep. The emotional and physical aftermath of SCAD was like being cracked open, raw and uncertain. The business I had built over the last fifteen years was slowly sinking because I couldn't keep up with how I was feeling every day. Most days, just getting through was hard enough. I lost my sport, my body, and now my business. Everything was falling apart.

And beneath all of that—the exhaustion, the fear, the spiraling identity—was the weight of mom guilt. I couldn't attend my sons' football games because I could barely stay on my feet. The sidelines that once felt like joy now felt like heartbreak.

During that hospital stay, one moment truly shattered me: FaceTiming Magnus to tell him I couldn't chaperone his first field trip. He was only six. The second the words left my mouth, his face crumpled, and he started bawling—his little voice raw with sadness and desperation. I had never heard that kind of cry from him before, and it gutted me.

I couldn't reach through the screen. I couldn't scoop him into my arms the way I always had. All I could do was watch as his heartbreak poured out, while mine did too.

That moment haunted me—not just for what I missed, but for how helpless I felt. How do you explain to a little boy why his mom, who was always strong and present, suddenly couldn't show up?

Maybe you've missed a moment you longed to be part of, and it broke you. I get it. Sometimes the weight of motherhood is invisible—but unbearably heavy.

I couldn't even say the word "heart attack" for months. Saying it felt like acceptance—and I wasn't ready. I was living in the aftermath, doing the healing, taking the medications. But saying it out loud made it too real.

My boys knew something had happened to my heart. They saw me move more slowly, wince more, rest more. But I couldn't give it a name—not yet. Watching their eyes take in my limitations was almost more painful than the chest pressure itself.

I tried to stay strong for them. Smiled when they were looking. Held it all in. And then I'd close the door to my bedroom or bathroom and cry. I hated that they saw me like this. They were used to being wrapped in my arms, picked up, and spun around. Now I couldn't even lift them. I felt like my body had betrayed me. I was angry, not just at the diagnosis, but at what it had stolen.

But over time, I stopped fighting it. I stopped pushing away the grief and started listening to it. Letting it be a part of me—not the end of me.

The Search for Answers

One of the hardest parts about the weeks and months after I came home was the lack of information they had about SCAD and even women's heart health in general. I was on a mission to research and find whatever I could—but I fell short time and time again.

How could we not know more about this? I quickly found out that it's the #1 heart attack in women under 50 who are otherwise healthy.

I joined every online SCAD support group I could find. I fell into rabbit holes reading posts from survivors—women with scars down their chests from open heart surgery, others who'd suffered second and third dissections. I saw messages from heartbroken family members who'd lost someone to SCAD.

It was like standing on the edge of a cliff with no map and no net—just sorrow, confusion, and a desperate need for answers.

Maybe you've felt this way too. Like you were drowning in questions and coming up empty. Like no matter how hard you searched, you kept running into walls. You were desperate for answers, but they never came. And somewhere along the way, the hope you started with began to fade.

I know that feeling. I've lived it. I want you to know you're not alone in it.

The bright spot? In that storm, I connected with incredible women whose stories mirrored mine. We bonded instantly. That helped.

So did the little things at home that reminded me I wasn't alone. One of those things was my boys taking turns helping me with my daily blood pressure checks. They took their job seriously, carefully wrapping the cuff around my arm and pressing the button with focused determination.

Giving them that task gave them a way to participate in my recovery—to feel like they were part of the healing, not just watching it happen. It gave us small moments of connection, and it helped all of us feel just a little more in control. But I was still turning over every stone, searching for people, doctors, anyone who could look me in the eye and tell me: "You're going to be okay."

I hadn't found my answer yet. But I hadn't stopped looking either. I didn't know where the next step would come from; I only knew I had to keep asking, keep knocking, keep moving. Even if it was through tears. Even if it was through fear. Because somewhere in all of this, I still believed healing was possible. And I was determined to find it.

This chapter of my life wasn't glamorous. It was raw and real and humbling. But if you're in a similar chapter—rebuilding, reaching, questioning—let this be your reminder: healing is rarely linear, but it's always possible.

You don't have to do it perfectly. You just have to keep going. Even now, I'm learning that healing isn't a box to be checked—it's a winding road I still walk, some days stronger than others.

♡ From My Heart to Yours

If you're in the thick of it—the fog of healing, the blur of fear, the ache of missing your old life—You're not behind. You're exactly where healing begins.

Recovery doesn't always look like progress. Sometimes it looks like lying awake at 2 a.m. with your hand over your heart, wondering if you'll make it through. Sometimes it looks like crying in silence, pretending to be strong for your kids, your partner, your world. But I see you. I know that quiet bravery.

If you've ever felt like no one understands what you're going through, you're not alone. I searched for answers, for hope, for a sign that someone had walked this path before me—and now, I hope this chapter becomes that sign for you.

You are not your diagnosis. You are not the body that betrayed you. You are the soul still rising from it all.

One step. One heartbeat. One breath at a time.

PART THREE

REBUILDING

The Stillness That Steadies.
The Ache That Teaches.
The Quiet Rise Of Something New.

CHAPTER 9

The Brave Kind of Stillness

*"Our greatest glory is not in never falling,
but in rising every time we fall."*
–Confucius

When Trying Feels Like a Wall

Have you ever felt as though no matter how hard you tried to find a solution, you kept running into walls? That every effort ended with you collapsing at the end of the day, exhausted from the pushing and the hoping?

That's what recovery felt like for me. I wish I could say I came home and slowly started to feel better. But the truth is, I didn't. Not for a long time. I actually felt worse.

The days blurred together. Mornings came, but I didn't feel rested. Nights were sleepless, full of chest pressure, phantom symptoms, and racing thoughts. I'd wake up in a panic, soaked in sweat, heart racing, dizzy, convinced I was having another SCAD. Sometimes I took my blood pressure three times before the boys were even out of bed.

I had referrals, test results, medication bottles—but no clarity. I searched high and low for doctors who understood SCAD, gathering records, making appointments, following every lead I could. But each attempt felt like another wall.

My energy was gone. Getting out of bed took me an hour most days. I had to set my alarm extra early just to give myself enough time to manage my body and the pain before getting the boys ready for school. My body moved like it had aged decades overnight—every joint stiff, every movement slow. And when I finally sat up, it felt like my heart was still left behind in the bed.

I spent most of my days lying down, trying to conserve whatever I could so I could be present for the boys when they got home from school. I measured out my strength in minutes, not hours—sometimes in breaths. Walking upstairs felt like climbing a cliff. Making their school lunches felt like a marathon.

But still, I tried to hold on to any routine that made me feel like myself. I would see my sneakers and gym bag sitting untouched in the corner, and it ached my heart. They were reminders of a life that felt like it belonged to someone else now. I missed it. I missed *me*. I was so angry at my body and felt like it had betrayed me. How could it when I had cared for it so well? It felt like betrayal.

Maybe you've had a time like that where simply existing takes everything you've got. Where you're doing your best to hold your life together with the frayed strings of your own will. It's a lonely kind of survival, but even there, you're holding more strength than you know.

I tried to smile for my boys, to answer work emails, to keep moving—but inside, it was like doing life through a thick, invisible fog. I journaled. I prayed. I searched. I called doctors and chased referrals. I did everything I knew to do.

And still, I kept running into walls. But somewhere inside, I knew I had to keep trying anyway.

The Search That Shattered Me

I had joined online SCAD support groups to feel less alone. But those pages were a mixed bag of hope and heartache.
I would spiral down rabbit holes, reading stories of women just like me—who had been young, vibrant, and healthy—now scared, confused, and searching for answers.

Stories of women who faced second, third, even fourth SCADs.
New mothers nursing newborns while trying to heal.
Women who endured open-heart surgery just to survive.
Women who buried their mothers, sisters, daughters, best friends—lost to something no one ever warned them about.
Women begging for doctors who would simply listen.
Healthy women, athletes, stripped of everything they once knew.

And still... they were fighting to be seen.

And reading all of it—the grief, the strength, the unanswered questions—began to wear on me. I wanted connection, but some days it only added to the weight.

I would close my laptop or put down my phone, with my heart sore and a sadness I couldn't name.

These were real women, living real fear.

And suddenly, my own story felt like it was floating in the same sea of uncertainty.

I wasn't just witnessing it, I was in it.

And the more I read, the more I realized I wasn't just craving connection, I was craving a path forward.

Somewhere between the grief and the unknown, I knew I had to *do* something.

I had to move, even if just an inch.

Around that time, I was finally cleared to start cardiac rehab.

Searching for Someone Who Knew

Starting cardiac rehab is different for every patient. For me, I was cleared about a month after. I thought I was ready—but at the same time, I wasn't.

I tried different centers. Multiple times.

Just trying to find one that was open was its own battle. So many had shut down after COVID, or weren't taking new patients.

Let me get this straight: cardiovascular disease is the leading cause of death in women and men—in the entire world—and I can't find a single rehab center that knows how to work with someone like me?

A woman. A survivor. A human being who just needed help getting her life back.

Ask me how this felt.

It was maddening. Disorienting. Like screaming into the void while the world carried on.

I filled out the paperwork, booked appointments, and showed up with hope—hope that maybe someone could help me get back to myself, even just a little. But each time, I left after the first visit. The disappointment was gutting. Different centers, same experience.

I would sit down with the staff, only to hear some version of, "We don't know that much about SCAD," or "We haven't worked with anyone like you."

I would walk out of each new appointment—
the slow walk to my car with tears streaming down my face.
Sitting in the front seat, staring out the windshield in devastation.
I was lost. I felt like I was losing hope. Like I was going to die,
and no one would be able to help me.

It was the most deflating feeling I'd ever had. I don't think I'd ever felt so alone—not even as my younger self.

Have you ever felt like that?

TORN HEART

Where you were searching high and low for help
for something you needed so deeply
and just couldn't find it?

Each time, I felt a wave of helplessness wash over me.
I wasn't just looking for care.
I was looking for understanding.

And I kept walking away empty.
Walking away in exhaustion.
It took all I had to even make it to those appointments.

And the scariest part was that some days, I didn't want to keep trying.

Some days, the sadness wrapped around me so tightly
I couldn't see a way out.

But I kept going.

Even when I didn't want to.

I had been asking everyone—my family, friends, anyone who might have a lead on hospitals that truly saw women and specialized in heart care. My voice was steady, but inside, I was quietly pleading. I needed someone to help me find what I wasn't sure even existed.

A Thread of Light

And then, the text came.

"Have you seen this?"

It was from my cousin, and it held more than just a link—it held possibility.

The Corrigan Minehan Heart Center at Massachusetts General Hospital—just thirty minutes from me. Within it is a Women's Heart Health Program led by some of the top cardiologists in the country.

Finally, something felt different.

I sat still, the phone glowing in my hand. And for the first time in a long time, I exhaled. Not in fear. But in something that felt like hope.

What I didn't know yet—couldn't have known—was that this search, this click, would lead me to one of the most pivotal discoveries of my entire recovery. But that part came later.

I reread the words over and over. Was it real? Could it be? How did I not know about this sooner?

It felt like a thread of light. Something real. Something close.

For the first time in weeks, I didn't just feel hopeful—I felt seen. I felt like maybe, just maybe, someone out there would understand this mess I was living in. That someone might know how to help me climb out of it. It didn't fix everything, but it reminded me that I wasn't out of options. There was still a road forward.

I couldn't dial the number fast enough. My hands were shaking, not with fear this time, but with the spark of *finally*. Finally, a place that might understand. Then, I saw it on my computer screen:

SCAD Clinic. An actual SCAD Clinic—dedicated to patients like me. For the first time in weeks, I felt a jolt of possibility.

I pictured getting in quickly. Maybe they'd have an opening next week. Maybe someone would hear the urgency in my voice. Maybe they'd say, "Yes, we see SCAD patients all the time. Come in."

But that's not how it went.

When someone finally answered, I was met with kindness—and a waitlist. A long one.

Three months. My breath caught. My heart sank.

Three months? I didn't feel like I had three minutes. My body was still in crisis. My mind was unraveling by the hour. But what did I expect?

A miracle? A shortcut through a system that moves slowly even when your heart has split open?

Still, I didn't stop there. I did what I do: I moved.

I requested every record from every doctor I had seen. Hospital reports. Test results. Imaging. I gathered it all like armor and sent it off like a warrior preparing for battle. I made sure they had *everything*. And I didn't just wait, I made sure I was on every cancellation list. I followed up by email. I called. I checked in. Again and again and again.

Each time I reached out, I felt like I was whispering a prayer into the system: *Please, let there be a way in sooner.*

And then, one day, the email came.

A cancellation. A rescheduling. A miracle.

My appointment had been moved up. No longer months away—it was now just weeks. *Weeks.* I could barely believe it.

Relief bloomed in my body—not fear this time, but something gentler. Something sacred.

This time, it was hope.

This time, it was joy.

I was going to be seen.

It was happening. I had a date, a time, a place.

All those weeks of waiting, pushing, praying—they led here.

This was my chance. And I wasn't going to waste it.

I was ready. I looked up the name of the cardiologist I had been scheduled with, and instantly, something in me lit up.

A woman. Already, I felt seen.

And then I saw her credentials:
Assistant Professor of Medicine at Harvard Medical School.
Associate Physician in Cardiology at Massachusetts General Hospital.
Medical Director of the Heart Center at Mass General Waltham.

Oh. My. Goodness.

This wasn't just an appointment.
This was the moment I started to believe I might actually be cared for—
by someone who *got it.*

I didn't know yet what her presence would mean.
I just knew I was finally stepping into a room where maybe…
just maybe… I wouldn't have to explain or convince.

I could finally get to just be a patient. A woman. A heart survivor.
And be heard.

The Place That Saw Me

It felt like Christmas morning. I had been counting down the days, crossing them off like a child waiting for something magical. That appointment—that place—had become a beacon. In a season where everything felt out of control, this gave me something to hold onto. Something that resembled hope.

That week leading up to the visit, I was sleeping more than ever—sometimes ten hours a night—and still waking up drained. My body was in recovery mode. But my mind wouldn't stop spinning. I replayed every possible scenario, every question I needed to ask, every answer I prayed to hear. I was nervous, but more than anything, I was ready. Ready to be seen. Ready to feel like someone, somewhere, could help me.

It felt like my last hope. And I was holding on to it with everything I had.

The day of my visit, my mom came with me. She's my rock. Both of my parents are incredible—loving, supportive, and steady in a world that felt so fragile. I know how lucky I am to have them. Their strength has always been my foundation, and in moments like these, it held me up even when I didn't feel steady.

I remember her pulling into the parking garage, surrounded by the chaos of Boston—crosswalks buzzing, cars honking, people moving fast, while I moved slowly. We circled the levels again and again, searching for a space. It felt like everything was loud, busy, impatient—the opposite of what I needed.

And then came the part I dreaded most: the walk.

From the car to the elevator. From the elevator to the sidewalk. Across buildings. Through hallways. Step by slow step.

I could've asked my mom to drop me off at the entrance. But I didn't. Maybe I was still trying to prove something to myself. That I could do this. That my body still worked. That I was still strong.

But the truth was: every few steps, I had to stop and catch my breath. My legs felt like anchors. My chest felt heavy. I was exhausted before we even got inside.

She stayed close. I don't even think she knew how hard it was for me.
But I made that walk.
Breathless. Slowly.
Holding on to my mom's strength when mine wasn't enough.

I still couldn't believe I hadn't thought of MGH sooner. One of the top hospitals in the world—practically in my backyard. But that's what the fog of survival does. It clouds even the most obvious paths.

Have you ever been searching so hard for something, only to realize it was right in front of your face the whole time? Sometimes clarity doesn't come with logic—it comes with timing. With grace. With the moment you're finally ready to see it.

The waiting room was packed. At least five receptionists behind glass partitions, patients being checked in, buzzers being handed out like it was a crowded restaurant. I looked around—over 30 people waiting. And I instantly felt the familiar ache of not belonging.

I was wearing bright colors. My big blonde hair was up in a half ponytail with a flower in it. I looked young and bubbly—and completely out of place.

Most of the people in the waiting room were elderly. One gentleman was in a wheelchair with an oxygen tank. Another had a monitor strapped to his chest and a walker in front of him.

I felt like everyone looked at me when my buzzer went off. Their eyes seemed to ask the questions I already carried inside me: *How could she be here? What's wrong with her?*

Inside the exam room, I met with a cardiac fellow first. She was kind, calm, and warm. She spoke like she already knew me. She did. She knew my case, had reviewed my files, and even told me they had discussed it on a Zoom call with other cardiologists. I couldn't believe it. I wanted to cry. I did cry.

She asked me gently, "Would you like to see the video of your cardiac catheterization? The moment we could see the SCAD?"

Wait—what? No one had offered me that before.

And in true Tara fashion—part heart warrior, part wellness nerd—I lit up:
"Yes, absolutely. Show me everything."

She turned the screen toward me and pressed "play."
There it was. *My* heart.
I watched as the dye flowed through the artery, steady and rhythmic.
And then—a pause.
She pointed. "See this? Right here—that's where the dissection appears."

I leaned in, mesmerized.
The pulsing. The contrast dye.
The tear—not as an explosive moment, but as a silent wound, now made visible.
A break in the vessel. A rupture in the rhythm.
And in that still, glowing image, I saw the truth my body had been screaming all along.

It was surreal. To sit in a chair and *watch* my own heart's injury.
Like looking through a window into the most private pain I had ever lived through.
I didn't know whether to cry or cheer—maybe both.
Because for the first time, I wasn't just *feeling* my trauma.
I was *witnessing* it.

Maybe you've had a moment like that—
when your invisible pain was finally reflected back to you in something concrete.
And suddenly, your story wasn't just valid…
It was real.

TORN HEART

And it mattered.

Then Dr. Sarah Tsiaras walked in.
She was smart, clear, compassionate—and she made me feel safe.

But more than that… she looked at me like she *saw* me.

Not just as a chart.
Not just as a diagnosis.
But as a whole human who had been holding it together with threads and grit.

And I saw her too.

She had this petite frame—lean, agile, the kind of body that moved with purpose.
Within seconds, I just *knew*: she was an athlete. A runner, maybe.
She carried that quiet discipline I recognized in myself—that language of movement, of endurance.

In that instant, I didn't just feel safe—I felt connected.
I wanted to hug her.
To pour every ounce of gratitude and love still left in my aching body into her.
(And let's be honest—I think I actually did.)

I sat there and wondered—*does she even know what this means to me?*

Does she realize how many weeks I've spent searching for someone like her?
How many phone calls, referrals, and dead ends I've been through?

How many nights I cried myself to sleep, thinking no one would ever understand what was happening in my body?

I don't know if she knew—in that exact moment—that she was changing my life. But she was.

There's a kind of sacred power in being looked at with compassion by someone who has the knowledge to help you.
A kind of grounding that starts to settle the chaos.
Her presence was steady. Her words were calm. Her knowledge was deep.
But what moved me the most wasn't clinical—it was *human*.

She acknowledged what I'd been through.
Not just the SCAD, but the in-between. The invisible middle.
The part where I had been dismissed. The part where I had lost hope.

She listened to my story like it mattered. Like *I* mattered.

And I thought—do doctors know that they carry this kind of power?
That just one appointment, one moment, one glance that says, *I see you* can begin to stitch someone back together?

I wanted to freeze that moment—
the stillness in the room, the rising in my chest,
the feeling that I had finally landed somewhere safe.

For a breath of time, I let myself drift into hope—
hope that maybe *this* doctor would say something different.
Even though I'd heard the warnings before,
a quiet part of me still believed I might be the exception.
That *maybe* she would look at me and say,

TORN HEART

"You're strong. You're different. You'll be back."

That I could return to lifting.
That I could still compete.
That I could do sprints again,
crush HIIT workouts,
feel the fire of a hot yoga class as sweat poured and silence settled.
That I could step back into that fierce rhythm—
the one that had been my lifeline for more than thirty years.

Because it wasn't just about movement.
It was about identity.
It was how I processed pain.
How I metabolized anxiety.
How I *stayed alive* when everything felt heavy.

Dr. T explained what they knew—
and what they didn't.

She named the possibilities.
Stress. Hormones. Hidden conditions.

But in the same breath—
the hardest truth.

They don't really know why SCAD happens.
Not yet.
Not enough.

The causes lived more in theories than in facts.
And that uncertainty

weighed almost as heavy,
as the diagnosis itself.

And as she spoke—calm, clear, and kind—
I felt that flicker of hope quietly dissolve.

Her words weren't harsh.
They were loving. Steady. Direct.
She was protecting my future—
even as she was helping me say goodbye to a piece of my past.

And as her words settled,
tears began to pour down my face.

I turned to my mom beside me—
the one who had witnessed every high and low—
and she grabbed my hand,
squeezed it tight,
and didn't let go.

There were no words.
But in that squeeze, there was permission to grieve.
To exhale.
To let the loss *be real.*

What I didn't realize, sitting in that exam room with swollen eyes and a hopeful heart,
was that this moment would mark the beginning of something much bigger.

TORN HEART

A long, winding journey of shedding, grieving, and slowly rebuilding the woman I thought I had lost.

It was the start of learning how to let go—
of who I had been,
of how I had measured strength,
of what I thought healing was supposed to look like.

But it was also the beginning of something sacred.
Of becoming the woman I was always meant to be.

That day at MGH was more than an appointment.
It was a reclamation.
It was the moment I stopped begging to be seen—
because someone finally looked at me and said,
"You matter. And we're going to walk this with you."

If you're reading this and you've been dismissed,
misunderstood, or searching for someone who gets it,
I hope this chapter breathes belief into you.

The right care exists.
The right people exist.
And when you find them, it can change everything.

MGH changed everything for me.

I didn't know it yet—but some of these people would help me put language to my pain. They saw my story inside the scar.

This wasn't just part of my story.

This was the story—
of hope rediscovered,
of healing reignited,
of what's possible when the right people hold your heart
with both science and soul.

♡ From My Heart to Yours

If you're in a season that feels like standing still—where you're waiting, aching, or wondering if anything will ever shift—I want you to know:

Stillness doesn't mean failure. And it doesn't mean you're broken.

Sometimes, the bravest thing you can do is *stay*.
Stay with the ache.
Stay with the questions.
Stay with your breath—even when every part of you wants to disappear.

This chapter of my life didn't come with grand victories or loud triumphs.
It came with quiet persistence.
With small, sacred refusals.
Refusing to give up.
Refusing to stop searching.
Refusing to believe that this was where my story ended.

If that's where you are right now—in the long middle—I see you.

And I promise, your turning point might be closer than you think.

The right person.
The right path.
The right moment.
It *can* find you—even here.

Heart Truths We Can't Ignore

The reality for women—especially women like me—is this:

- Cardiovascular disease (CVD) is the leading cause of death for women in the U.S., responsible for one in every three female deaths.
- SCAD (spontaneous coronary artery dissection) is a leading cause of heart attacks in women under 50—especially healthy, fit women with no risk factors.
- Women are 50% more likely than men to be misdiagnosed after a heart attack.
- 80% of women miss the early signs of a heart attack.
- Only 38% of women know that heart disease is their greatest health threat.
- Just 12% of cardiologists are women.
- Most cardiac rehab programs were designed with male patients in mind.
- CVD is the leading cause of maternal mortality in the United States.
- Chronic stress is a silent contributor to heart disease in women—especially caretakers, mothers, and high performers.
- Emotional trauma can double a woman's risk of heart disease—and no one's talking about it.

- Black women are particularly at risk—more likely to develop heart disease and less likely to receive timely treatment.

These aren't just statistics.
They are lives.
They are stories.
They are reasons to speak up.

(Source: American Heart Association, Johns Hopkins Medicine, Harvard Women's Clinic, Mayo Clinic, and NIH data)

CHAPTER 10

Born from the Break

"Sometimes good things fall apart,
so better things can fall together."
–Marilyn Monroe

The Year That Reshaped Me

Maybe you're in your own season of healing right now. Maybe your break looked different than mine—a loss, a diagnosis, a dream unraveling—but still, here you are. Trying to find solid ground. If that's you, this chapter is for you.

The first full year of healing after my SCAD was one of the most intense chapters of my life. My body no longer felt like mine. My mind felt foreign, too. And yet, I was still a mom—with two boys watching me closely, learning not just how I survived… but how I lived.

Deep down, in the quiet corners of my spirit, I knew this was going to change me. I just didn't know how.

Have you ever felt like you were meant for something more—something bigger than your current reality—but you couldn't quite name it? Maybe you were blocked by your thoughts, or boxed in by time, money, or support.

For me, it was all of those things. My business was struggling, my energy was limited, and survival was still the priority. But there was a shift. I began to notice that things that used to rattle me no longer held the same weight. I was softening in some places, sharpening in others. I was living with more intention, more purpose, more reverence.

Every day, I crafted a new routine—small acts of care to keep me grounded. This was nothing new for me; I've always been someone who finds power in structure. But now, I was beginning to realize how much these practices could help others, too. That's when **The M.O.V.E. Method**™ was born. (More on that in the next chapter—real, life-changing tools to help you shift from where you are.)

Rehab and Revelation

Now that I had found my hospital and my doctor at MGH, it was time to revisit cardiac rehab. After months of crushing disappointment searching for a facility that could truly help me, a new door opened at MGH. And with that door came Nancy.

She was the cardiac rehab nurse from MGH who first called me over Zoom—and I swear she was heaven-sent. A nurse, yes, but also an anchor in the storm, an angel with a calm, steady soul who met me with the kind of compassion I hadn't even realized I needed. She had worked with other SCAD survivors and knew more about SCAD than any nurse I had met to date. Her presence marked the beginning of my rehab journey and the start of feeling safe in my healing.

Just getting to the rehab session was a commitment—an hour and a half each way with traffic. And the thought of making that kind of trip several times a week, while still healing, while running a business, while mothering... it overwhelmed me.

But because of Nancy, I went.

The first day I walked in, I felt it—a shift. A softening. A sense that I was finally in the right place. I was still surrounded by the familiar stereotype of heart disease—older men, lined up in quiet rows, machines humming low as they walked or cycled with wires on their chests. But something about this place felt different.

I felt seen.

As I got hooked up to the monitors and stepped onto the treadmill beside them, I could feel their eyes on me. I was young. I was different. I didn't look like I belonged there. And maybe, in some ways, I didn't.

But then I tripped—just a little—and started laughing at myself. That moment broke the silence like sunlight cracking through a storm. They laughed with me.

Suddenly, we were talking. I began sharing parts of my story, and they listened—wide-eyed, open-hearted, quietly in awe. I wasn't just a patient to them. I was a reminder that heart disease doesn't always look the way we think it does.

I kept going. Week after week. And that place—that drive, those treadmills, those conversations—became a vital part of my healing.

Physically, yes. But also emotionally. It gave me a place to return to myself. To move without fear. To breathe without bracing.

I will forever be grateful for that time, for that room, for Nancy—and for the strange beauty of finding connection in the most unexpected places.

When the Ocean Didn't Heal Me

Jack and I had been taking the boys to the Cape for years—a tradition stitched into our summers. It was always my happy place—the ocean, beach, the salt air, the soft rhythm of waves meeting sand. I loved the packing chaos, the coolers, the beach chairs, the pails, and shovels. I carried it all. Fast. Strong. Grounded.

But this first summer after my SCAD… I couldn't carry anything.

Not physically. Not emotionally.

My heart had torn, and everything that once felt light now felt impossibly heavy.

One of my best friends, Jenn, lived on the Cape during the summers. We'd been close for decades—first through fitness, then through motherhood, and every layer of life that followed. The kind of friend who shows up before you even ask. Our friendship had blossomed later in life, but it carried the weight of something timeless—the kind of bond that saves you quietly, daily, and makes you more yourself than you ever thought you could be.

I remember pulling up to the beach and sitting in the car for a moment too long. I knew what was ahead—the sun, the sand, the people. But also… the invisible weight. The embarrassment of not being able to haul a cooler. The guilt of needing help when I used to be the one helping everyone else.

Jenn would come running—every time. No questions. No judgment. Just arms reaching for the bags and the beach chairs and the grief I didn't know how to name yet. She carried it with me.

And that was everything.

Some people arrive in your story for a reason you can name. Others, like Jenn, arrive and change you in ways you can't. She didn't just carry the bags; she carried me through some of the heaviest seasons. Our friendship, though it blossomed later, became one of the greatest medicines in my healing—steady, saving, sacred.

By the next summer, I thought I'd feel more like myself again. I didn't.

One morning, Jenn and I went for a walk along the shoreline—something so simple, so healing in theory. But within minutes, I was winded. I had to keep stopping, catching my breath, whispering, "Just a minute."

She matched my pace without hesitation. Patient. Steady. Soft.

But inside, I felt like I was unraveling.
Like the strong woman I once was had been carried out with the tide.

Two summers. Same beach.
Different strengths.
Different woman.

And still—I was there.

Present. Healing. Becoming.

Sometimes healing doesn't look like peace.
It looks like walking the same shoreline with a slower breath.
It looks like showing up anyway.

Sometimes, the right people meet you exactly where you are—and that alone begins to heal you. Jenn was one of those people for me.

The Weight of Coming Back

Cardiac rehab helped me trust my body again. But stepping back into the gym was about something bigger: facing the identity I thought I had lost, and learning to meet the woman I hadn't yet recognized.

My return to the gym was emotional. I remember pulling my trucker hat low, trying not to make eye contact, as I stepped back into the place that once felt like home. Not my typical shoulders-back, head-held-high, strong-and-confident Tara. Just a woman trying to find her footing again—tender, unsure, and humbled.

This gym had once been my second home. My sanctuary. My extended family. Everyone knew me here. I was the girl who showed up every day, part of the rhythm and the community. And now, I was trying to hide. I could feel their eyes on me—watching me ease back in with movements so different from the woman they remembered. It felt like being on stage again, only this time it wasn't the same performance.

I saw women lifting weights, and tears stung my eyes. I missed her—the old me. But I was no longer chasing her. I was committed to meeting the new version of myself. And I was willing to do the work, however slow it needed to be.

At first, it was just stretching. A few minutes on the treadmill. Slow, gentle, deliberate movement. That was enough. And sweetly, my mom came with me. I think she was worried her overachieving daughter would push too hard, too fast. She wasn't wrong. But her presence brought comfort—a silent permission to go slow. We never used to work out together. I had always trained alone. But this season of recovery, we shared. And somewhere in that process, she found healing, too.

People started noticing us working out together and often would comment on how amazing it was to see a mother and daughter training side by side. When one of us showed up without the other, we'd often get asked, "Where's your gym partner?" It became a special rhythm between us—something sacred we didn't plan but deeply valued. It was a bond made not just of blood, but of breath and movement—a quiet, daily reminder that healing isn't always done alone.

Once the girl who stacked fourteen forty-five-pound plates on each side of the leg press—yes, over 600 pounds—now wasn't even supposed to lift a single one. When I finally felt ready to try the machines again, I didn't feel strong. I felt weak. Tired. Sad. Like I was a stranger inside my own body.

Then came a moment I'll never forget.

I stood at the leg press, staring at the weight left behind by someone else—just one forty-five-pound plate. A plate I used to throw around like it was nothing. And I had to ask someone to help me take it off.

Me.

The woman who used to move fourteen of them without blinking. The one who would mutter under her breath, "Re-rack your weights," every time someone left theirs behind. My biggest gym pet peeve.

But now? I understood. In a way I never had before.

Some people can't pick them up.

And now I was one of them.

It wasn't easy to ask for help. It stung. My pride did too. Just months earlier, I was pressing those same plates like they were five pounds. I had been the one others looked to. The one moving with purpose.

I'd been in the gym since I was 16. It was my comfort zone. My sanctuary. The place I knew who I was and what I could do.

And suddenly, it felt foreign. Unfamiliar. No longer safe.

I was scared. And I was lonely.

Some might say, "It's just weights. Just the gym." But it wasn't. Not to me. It was where I had built my strength—not just physically, but emotionally. It was where I reshaped my identity, one rep at a time. And now, I was being asked to return to that place—stripped down, starting from nothing.

And somehow… I did.

♡ From My Heart to Yours

I thought healing meant doing it alone, proving I was strong enough. But what I've learned is that sometimes, healing is shared. It's the people who meet you in hospital rooms, on shorelines, and beside weight racks. It's in those quiet bonds that I found myself again.

Maybe for you, healing won't look like pressing plates or walking beaches. Maybe it will be something quieter: catching your breath, asking for help, or letting someone carry the bags when you can't. Healing doesn't always look like victory. Sometimes it looks like simply showing up anyway.

Your growth isn't measured by speed, but by courage.

CHAPTER 11

The Bridge No One Sees

The Beat Between Heartbeats

"Owning our story and loving ourselves through that process is the bravest thing that we'll ever do."
—Brené Brown

The Long Middle

They don't talk about this part.

Not the comeback, not the collapse—
But the stretch in between.
The bridge.
The part where you're still standing,
but barely.

Where every breath is a decision.
Where faith feels like a whisper,
and strength isn't something you show—
it's something you *choose,* moment to moment.

TORN HEART

That season—the one I'm about to share—isn't behind me yet.
I'm still in it. Still crossing the bridge, one unsteady step at a time.
But even now, I'm learning that this middle place—
the place between no longer and not yet—
has lessons I couldn't have learned anywhere else.

When you're in a bridge season,
your body remembers the weight as it's carried—
not just as a memory, but as a message:
You are still here. You are still finding your way.

There was a time, not long ago,
when I was holding everything together with shaking hands.
The future was unclear.
And the mission I believed in felt farther away than I could reach.

I had already survived trauma, SCAD, burnout, and heartbreak.
But nothing prepared me for what it meant to rebuild *while still bleeding*.

There was no roadmap.
No applause.
Just quiet faith and exhausted hope.

That season didn't make headlines.
But it was where I met the deepest version of myself.
The woman who rose… even without proof that rising was possible.

This is the beat between heartbeats.
And it still lives in me.

The Weight We Carry in Silence

There's a kind of grief that comes when you want more—but can't yet see how to reach it.

Not the kind that knocks the wind out of you all at once,
but the slow, aching kind—
the kind that builds in the quiet moments when you let yourself dream, and then pull back, whispering, "But how?"

How do I build a new life while holding up the old one?
How do I chase a dream and still pay the bills?
How do I become *her*—the version of me I can feel rising?

I was still folding laundry, pretending not to notice the bills rising while the income slowed. Still pushing forward with half-hope, half-exhaustion—willing something to shift.

These are the questions so many women carry—
in the grocery aisle, on the bathroom floor, between meetings and bedtime stories. How do I reach it? The more I know I was made for?

They want more.
More purpose.
More money.
More impact.
More joy.
More room to breathe.
More time to *live*.

And yet… they're stuck.

TORN HEART

Not because they're lazy.
Not because they lack ambition.
But because fear—that ancient, familiar companion—whispers:

You can't have that.
You waited too long.
It's too late.
You'll never make it work.
You'll fail and then what?

And maybe that's where you are.
Or maybe you've been there before.
I know I have.

I want to help women believe again.
And maybe that's where you are.
Or maybe you've been there before.
I know I have.

I turned 48 and felt it like a pulse in my chest.
I've lived half my life.
And I want *so many things now.*

I want to speak on stages that matter.
To write words that outlive me.
To show my boys what it means to reinvent yourself when the world says stay small.
To build wealth from purpose—not just pressure.
To travel and feel wonder again.
To live—fully, freely, audaciously.

But no one tells you how hard the in-between is.

They show you the highlight reel.
Not the days when you stare at your laptop, wondering how you'll make it through the month.
Not the moments when you cry in the car because you're so damn tired of *almosts* and *not yets.*
Not the quiet decision to keep going—even when the world isn't clapping yet.

We carry that weight in silence.
Because we've been taught to.

But what if we didn't?

What if this is the most sacred part of all—
The season where we choose *us*—even when it's hard?

Before you move on, I invite you to pause.
What is your heart quietly asking for—even if it feels impossible?
Can you give it space to speak?

I asked myself that same question—not once, but over and over.
While the answers weren't always clear, they led me back to a deeper truth.

That truth met me not at my strongest, but at my most stripped down.
It began here…

The Ache of Identity Loss

When I first came home from the hospital, it didn't feel like a return. It felt like a reckoning.

I wasn't just trying to recover physically; I was trying to reconcile the version of me I had always known... with the one I barely recognized.

The CEO. The high-performer. The mom who ran a business and a household without missing a beat.

That woman had disappeared into blood pressure cuffs, pill bottles, and follow-up scans.

And the athlete in me—the disciplined, unstoppable, relentless woman who found freedom in motion—was gone too.

I couldn't lift weights.

I couldn't run.

I couldn't even walk up the stairs without feeling like I might break.

I had worked so hard to build a body that could protect me.

And now it felt like that very body had betrayed me.

There was grief in that.

Grief for the woman I used to be.

Grief for the goals I had set and the timelines I had drawn.

Grief for the routines, the energy, the fire that had fueled me.

Maybe you've felt that too.

Maybe you've always been the strong one.

The dependable one.

The one who holds it all together—even when you're falling apart inside.

Maybe strength is your default, because softness never felt safe.

Maybe you *have* to be in that role.

Or maybe, like me, you learned to put yourself there—because it felt like the only option.

But let me say this:
Riding in your purpose, letting down the walls that restrict you, doesn't lessen your strength—it refines it.
It makes you more powerful, not less.
More whole, not less worthy.
Because true strength isn't just about what you carry.
It's about what you choose to lay down.
It's about allowing yourself to dream again.
To believe again.
To hope—even when everything in you wants to shut down.

And if you haven't felt that spark yet—if hope still feels far away—know this: you're not alone. I didn't feel it at first, either.

But there was also something else.
Not right away.
Not in the hospital bed.
Not even in those first uncertain months.

But slowly—
like light through a crack,
a glimmer began to form.
A whisper.
A quiet sense that maybe this wasn't an ending—
it was the beginning of a different kind of becoming.
That maybe I hadn't lost everything…
maybe I was being invited to build something deeper.

Not based on muscle or metrics or business milestones—
but on meaning.

So I sat in that ache.
I let it teach me what striving never could.
And I began—slowly, painfully—to ask a new question:

What if this version of me—the one still healing, still uncertain, still finding her breath—was enough?

When the Fire Changed

Grief lived in my chest that year—sharp and aching. I'd grip my heart, not just from the SCAD, but from the emotional wreckage it left behind. I missed who I was. But I have always been relentless. And this was no different—it just had to be different.

By mid-year, I felt that spark growing. My recruiting business was barely standing, and I was trying to keep it alive, balancing motherhood, healing, and the identity I had spent nearly twenty-plus years building.

It wasn't just a job. It was mine. My creation. My legacy. But something inside had shifted. The fire that once drove me had quieted. It wasn't that I didn't care—I cared deeply. But the urgency had transformed. What once felt like purpose now felt like pressure. And in its place grew a longing for something more expansive. More heart-centered. More aligned with the woman I was becoming.

If you're struggling to let go of who you once were—I get it. I was too. But surrender isn't giving up. It's making space. It's the bravest kind of trust. *I missed who I was. I missed what I had to let go of.* But something deeper was beginning to rise in me. My heart was pulling me somewhere new.

When Becoming Asks Everything

There's power in telling the truth—even when it terrifies you.

So here's mine:

I wasn't just recovering from an artery dissection in my heart—a condition few had even heard of. I was watching the version of me I had spent years building… begin to drown.

For nearly two decades, I had built a thriving recruiting business from the ground up. I had always been strong, strategic, successful—the one who made things happen. But suddenly, none of it felt sustainable. Not because I didn't care, but because the world had changed—and I had changed.

My business began to slip—slowly at first, and then all at once.
The economy was tightening. Clients were freezing budgets.
And I was still trying to hold it all together with trembling hands and a healing heart.

I would wake up, open my inbox, and see hundreds of messages from people desperate for work. And I felt their weight, because I was carrying my own. I was a mother trying to provide. A woman trying to keep the lights on. A heart survivor navigating the uncertainty of survival while still showing up, still hoping for the next client.

TORN HEART

Some might see that as a fall.
But I don't.
I see it as strength.

Because growth doesn't happen when everything is easy.
It happens when you keep moving anyway.
When you make the hard choice to believe in your future—
even when the present feels unbearable.

So I made a decision.
One I could barely afford—emotionally or financially.

But I made it anyway.

I said yes to the new path.

I went to events when I didn't feel ready.
I hired coaches when the budget was already stretched.
I joined mastermind groups, networking calls, and community circles.
I told myself, *I am not giving up.*
Not now. Not ever.

That didn't mean I didn't cry in my car.
Didn't doubt myself in the middle of the night.
Didn't wonder how I would make it through another month.

But somewhere deep in my soul, I knew:
This new life I was building—this voice I was finding—was worth it.

And that's what I want to tell you:
No matter where you are, it doesn't have to be where you stay.

You can begin again at 48.
At 58.
At any moment, your heart whispers: *There's more.*

You can rise from the version of yourself you thought you had to cling to—and become the one you were always meant to be.

Even if your voice shakes.
Even if your bank account is empty.
Even if you're terrified.

Especially then.

Because *that* is where the real becoming begins.

♡ **From My Heart to Yours**

If you're standing on a bridge between who you were and who you're becoming, I want you to know this:

You are not lost.
You are in motion.

Even when it feels like nothing is changing, *you are changing*. With every brave decision, every quiet tear, every moment you choose not to give up—
you are becoming the woman you were always meant to be.

It's okay if you're scared.
It's okay if you're stretched.
It's okay if you still don't know exactly how this ends.

Because some of the most beautiful chapters of your story will be the ones no one ever saw coming—
not even you.

Keep going, love.
The beat between heartbeats means your story isn't over.
It's just beginning.

I didn't know it then, but everything I was surviving—and every choice to keep going—was shaping a new path.

A framework.

A way forward I would one day name… M.O.V.E.

CHAPTER 12

The M.O.V.E. Method™
My Framework for Growth

*"The journey doesn't begin when life breaks you.
It begins when you decide not to stay broken."*
–Anonymous

Born from the Break. Built to Reclaim.

The M.O.V.E. Method™ was born in the middle of my unraveling. Not because I had all the answers, but because I knew the hardest choices are often the ones that change everything.

It's not a system I pulled from a book. It's a rhythm I found in my bones—clear, simple, powerful pillars to help you move through grief, identity shifts, burnout, heartbreak, and the hollow ache of starting over.

Each letter of M.O.V.E. is more than a step. It's a pillar. Something steady to lean on. Something sacred to rise from. These pillars unfold in their own rhythm. You'll revisit some; others will take longer. All of them will hold you.

Whether you're healing from illness, trauma, change, or the slow loss of yourself... this method is here to meet you exactly where you are.

M.O.V.E. stands for:

- **Manage** what you can control
- **Overcome** what holds you back
- **Value** the lessons inside the struggle
- **Evolve** into the version of yourself you were always meant to be

I know at first glance these pillars might seem almost too simple. Maybe even silly. They're the kinds of things we take for granted—and because they seem so small, we often don't do them. But that's where the shift happens. When practiced with intention, these simple choices work together to create a system that can change how your body and spirit feel every single day. And I know—because I am living proof of it.

And let's be honest—and I say this with all my love—you've already tried it the other way, haven't you? The pretending. The pushing. The striving. The surviving. Can you honestly say it feels good? Or is there a part of you that knows—you could feel better? That you *deserve* to feel better? This is where that begins.

This isn't a race. It's a remembering. A way forward that doesn't ask for perfection—only presence. Let it meet you in the stillness, in the chaos, in the aching space between who you were and who you're becoming.

This is the method I created when moving forward felt impossible—and the one that helped me rise, not back, but forward.

Before we begin, I want to share why this work means so much to me—and why it might mean something to you, too.

Before the Framework: Why This Matters

Because survival isn't enough.
Because so many of us are walking around looking "fine,"
but silently falling apart inside.
Because healing doesn't happen by accident—it happens when we start to move, on purpose.
Because no one hands us the roadmap after the breakdown—
we have to build it ourselves.
And I want to help you build yours.

I believe we each carry gifts the world needs—
not despite our pain, but often because of it.
I believe we can become the most honest, empowered version of ourselves
at any moment—even in the middle of the mess.
And I believe that when we care for our mind, body, and soul together,
we don't just heal our hearts—we change our lives.

The Choice to M.O.V.E.

One of the most powerful realizations we can have is this:
When life brings us to our knees, we still have a choice.
YOU have a choice.
You can stay exactly where you are—stuck, safe, surviving.
Because let's be honest: even pain can feel comfortable when it's familiar.
Or… you can M.O.V.E.

When I say "move," I'm not just talking about action—
I'm talking about a **movement.**
A **mindset.**
A **map.**

M.O.V.E. became the framework that pulled me out of the darkest chapters of my life and into the one I'm writing now.

It's more than a method.
It's a soul map—a way home to yourself.
It was born from survival,
but it grew from intention.

From the moments I wanted to give up, but didn't.
From the breath I took instead of the breakdown.
From every choice to show up—messy, real, and still moving.

This didn't come from theory.
It came from my life.
And now I want to share it with you—
not as a formula, but as a lifeline.

Let it meet you where you are.
Let it walk with you, the way it walked with me.

This isn't just a framework.
And it can change your life—and if you let it, it will.
It's how I survived the trauma.
The unraveling. The grief.
It's how I returned to my life with purpose—not just persistence.
A tree cannot grow upward until its roots are grounded deep in the earth.

This is your grounding.
This is your invitation to rise.

And now... let's begin.

♦ Step 1: MANAGE—Take Control of What You Can

Anchor yourself in what is within your reach.
Even when the storm howls, you still get to steer the ship.

This is where we start. The Manage pillar is about grounding yourself in the moment. These are the tools you can use today—even in survival mode. M is immediate. M is accessible. This is my favorite of the four—and the most foundational.

Because when life feels like it's spiraling, there's one truth I hold onto: **I still have power.** Maybe not over the world... but over my next choice.

Every day, we are faced with thousands of decisions.
And while we can't control everything, we can manage what we do have influence over—and that is where healing begins.

I had zero control over my SCAD heart attack.
Zero control over the ER that dismissed me,
the medications they gave me, and the heavy, layered healing that followed.

But when I came home?
That's where my power returned. I realized that I DID have control of many things.

I chose the food I ate.
I chose what I watched, listened to, and let into my space.
I chose how I spoke to myself—and whether I believed I was healing or hopeless.
I chose softness when my instinct was to push.

And when I couldn't choose much...
I still chose breath.

That's the moment I reclaimed my power.

Here's the deeper truth I've come to understand:
Even the smallest physical choice—a sip of water, a step outside, a single deep breath—is a message to your nervous system that you are safe. That you are home. That you are still here.

It's not about fixing everything. It's about tuning in. To your body. To your rhythm. To your yes and your no.

Some days, that might look like a walk. Other days, it might look like rest. Managing isn't about control—it's about connection.
To what's real.
To what's needed.
To you.

Here are some of the things you *can* manage right now:

- Your mindset
- Your response (even if you can't control the trigger)
- The food and drink you nourish your body with
- The media you consume (what you watch, listen to, scroll through)

- The energy you allow into your life—especially through the people around you

Healing doesn't always look heroic.
Sometimes it looks like choosing differently—in the middle of your same old day.
Sometimes it looks like breath.
A moment of stillness.
A quiet boundary.
A pause before you respond.

Even the smallest choice can spark something new.
A shift.
A return.
A remembering that you are not powerless—you're in progress.
One breath, one step, one moment at a time.

> 🌀 **Reader Reflection Prompt:**
>
> What's one small thing you can take control of today?
>
> What's something you can let go of that isn't yours to carry?

M.O.V.E. in Real Life: MANAGE
What it looked like for me:
I turned off my phone for an hour.

What it might look like for you:

- Moving your body in a way that feels good—stretching, walking, or dancing—just to feel alive again
- Choosing silence instead of scrolling
- Drinking a glass of water when your mind feels chaotic
- Preparing nourishing meals
- Saying "I need five minutes"—and taking them
- Noticing one thing around you that brings ease

Healing starts in the tiniest shift.

Don't wait for the perfect moment—begin with the next breath.

♦ Step 2: OVERCOME—Face the Obstacle Directly

Stand eye to eye with what scares you.
Don't run—rise. The only way through is through.

This is the pivot point. The Overcoming Pillar doesn't happen all at once—it often begins in the smallest moments. A new decision. A different thought. A breath when you used to break.

It's not about never falling—it's about how you rise. This pillar invites you to shift. To challenge. To say: "Not this time."

You may feel resistance. That's okay. You're not failing—you're forging. Overcoming builds in layers. Honor every step.

Here's the truth:
You can't heal what you refuse to face.

You can't rise above what you keep pushing beneath the surface.
And I know how tempting it is to bury it, outwork it, pretend it doesn't matter. But buried pain doesn't disappear. It grows roots in the dark.

For most of my life, I believed being strong meant keeping it together. Powering through. Wearing a smile. Swallowing the ache. But SCAD shattered that illusion. I couldn't fake my way through a heart attack. I couldn't outrun fear or grief or the identity loss that came after.

The only way forward… was through.

And that's what OVERCOME means—
Not that you'll never feel fear.
But that fear no longer gets to drive the car.
It means turning toward the pain—not to conquer it, but to truly meet it.
Not with force, but with gentleness.
Not to fix everything, but to finally face what's real.

Sometimes overcoming is loud—
A big decision, a bold truth, a brave new step.
But often, it's quiet—
Getting out of bed. Making the call. Saying the words you've avoided.

Here's what facing the obstacle looked like for me:

- Saying the word "heart attack" out loud, even when my throat closed around it
- Asking for help when I didn't want to need it
- Accepting my limitations without losing my worth
- Telling my sons the truth—that Mom was still healing

- Letting myself cry. Not just once, but again and again, until the grief softened

Maybe you're in your own battle right now.
Maybe the obstacle is inside of you—self-doubt, burnout, shame. Or maybe it's something outside your control—a diagnosis, a loss, a detour you didn't choose.

Whatever it is, please know this:

You can't conquer what you won't confront.
But when you do? Even if you shake. Even if you cry.
That's where the real power begins.

Even naming the fear out loud can loosen its grip.
Even placing your hand on your chest and saying, "I see you, and I'm still here," is a kind of overcoming.

You don't have to roar.
Sometimes healing sounds like a whisper.

> **⊚ Reader Reflection Prompt:**
>
> What fear are you avoiding right now?
>
> What would it look like to face it with kindness, not judgment?

M.O.V.E. in Real Life: OVERCOME
What it looked like for me:
"I told my truth, even when it trembled."

What it might look like for you:

- Asking for help without guilt
- Letting yourself cry instead of pushing it down
- Naming your fear out loud to a trusted friend
- Choosing the hard conversation instead of avoidance

Overcoming doesn't always look like conquering. Sometimes it looks like simply showing up.

◆ Step 3: VALUE—Find the Lesson in the Struggle

Honor the cracks, the mess, the ache—
Not as flaws, but as the sacred soil where growth begins.

The Value Pillar takes time. It's the quiet rebuild. The slow return to self-worth. You may not feel it at first—but trust me, it grows. And when it roots? Everything changes. It's one thing to survive something hard. It's another to turn that pain into meaning. To find value not in what happened to you, but in who you became because of it.

At first, I didn't want to learn anything from SCAD. I wanted it to go away. I wanted my old body, my old life, my old normal back.

But slowly, I began to see that the struggle itself was shaping me. It was humbling me. Softening me. Expanding me.

Pain has a way of revealing what really matters. And if you're willing to lean in—just a little—it can teach you things strength never could.

Here's what VALUE looked like in my life:

- Realizing my worth wasn't tied to my productivity or appearance
- Understanding that slowing down wasn't a failure—it was an act of wisdom
- Learning how to receive love and care, not just give it
- Deepening my connection with my children, not by doing more, but by being more present
- Rediscovering my voice—not as a recruiter, but as a woman with something to say

I remember one afternoon, sitting on the floor of my boys' playroom.
Toys were everywhere. The laundry was undone. I hadn't showered, and my chest still ached with fear.
But I was there—present, breathing, laughing.

We giggled. We acted silly. For a moment, I forgot to be afraid.
Then Maximus looked up and said,
"I love you, Mama."
At the same time, Magnus came up behind me and wrapped his little arms around my back—a quiet, wordless hug that said everything.

That moment pierced me in the best way.
They didn't need me to be busy or perfect or strong.
They just needed *me*.

That's when I realized: sometimes the value isn't in what we do—
it's in how fully we're willing to *be here*.
With our people. With our pain. With ourselves.

Maybe you're in a season where you're asking,
Why did this happen to me?

I don't have all the answers.
But I do know this:
There is always something to value in what you've lived through.

It might not show up right away. It might be subtle, quiet, buried deep under layers of grief. But it's there.

Even if it's just the strength you built by surviving. Even if it's knowing that you're still here.

◎ Reader Reflection Prompt:

What has life taught you through your hardest moments?

Is there something you've gained—perspective, patience, purpose—that you wouldn't have learned any other way?

M.O.V.E. in Real Life: VALUE
What it looked like for me:
I stopped apologizing for saying sorry.

What it might look like for you:

- Taking a break without explaining yourself
- Holding a boundary, even when it's uncomfortable
- Celebrating small wins instead of minimizing them
- Looking in the mirror and offering yourself kindness

Valuing yourself is the soil where your healing grows.

♦ Step 4: EVOLVE—Use the Experience to Grow

Let it all transform you.
You are not who you were—and that's the gift.
You're unfolding into someone braver.

The heart of this framework is the Evolve Pillar. However, evolution isn't an event. It takes time. This part can feel like a whisper before it becomes a roar. Let it be slow. Let it be sacred. Let it surprise you. This is the step that changes everything. Not just surviving. Not just learning. But *becoming*.

We don't walk through the fire to come out the same. We evolve so the fire has somewhere to go—so it becomes light for others.

For a long time, I thought evolving meant leaving behind who I was. But I've learned it's not about shedding your past, it's about integrating it. About honoring the girl who got you here, while allowing the woman you're becoming to lead.

Here's what EVOLVE looked like in my life:

- Accepting that my life would look different—and loving it anyway
- Finding joy in stillness, peace in imperfection
- Using my voice to advocate for women's heart health
- Sharing my story even when it scared me
- Building a new purpose from the pieces of my old one

I didn't get my "old life" back.
But I got something better: alignment.
And that alignment—heart, mind, mission—is what finally made me feel free.

You don't need to have it all figured out to evolve.
You don't need to know the whole path.
You just need to be willing to take the next honest step.

Evolution is not a destination.
It's a daily choice to keep growing—
even when it's hard,
even when it hurts,
even when it's quiet.

This isn't just something I teach—
It's something I return to daily.
I'm still evolving,
Still choosing this path when life feels uncertain.

After my SCAD, I clung to the business I had built with so much pride. I tried to keep it alive—even as the economy slowed and my energy shifted. I wasn't ready to let go.
For months, I resisted the change, afraid of what it might mean to walk away.

But purpose has a way of whispering louder when you stop drowning it out.

The more I said yes to what was calling me—writing, speaking, advocacy—the more I came home to myself. This wasn't just a new path.

It was a new version of me, one I didn't even know I was allowed to become.

There were real fears. Financial realities. Unknowns I still face.

But I no longer lead with scarcity. I lead with soul.
Because the truth is—nothing meaningful comes easy.
Growth doesn't arrive gift-wrapped.
It arrives when we choose to move, even when we're scared.

We don't evolve by avoiding the tension. We evolve by letting it stretch us. Just like the butterfly must press against the cocoon to rise.

◎ Reader Reflection Prompt:

Where in your life are you being called to evolve?

What part of you is ready to rise—even if you're still scared?

🦋 M.O.V.E. in Real Life: EVOLVE

What it looked like for me:
I walked away from something that used to define me.

What it might look like for you:

- Saying goodbye to a version of you that no longer fits
- Trying something new before you feel "ready"
- Letting yourself dream again—without limits
- Choosing softness instead of survival mode

Evolving doesn't erase who you were—it honors her, then grows beyond.

Want a simple one-page version of the M.O.V.E. Method™ you can keep close?

Download your free printable guide at:
👉 www.tarabenoit.com/MOVE

The Body Remembers—and the Body Heals

Before I ever had a name for what I was feeling,

my body knew.

It flinched before I admitted fear.
It tightened before I allowed grief.
It screamed in silence long before I ever found the words.

The body remembers what the mind tries to forget.

For years, I believed that strength lived in the grind—in the reps, the schedules, the pushing through. I wore physical discipline like armor. I didn't know then that sometimes the body isn't something to conquer… it's something to come home to.

After my heart attack, I didn't trust my body anymore. It had betrayed me. It broke me. Or so I thought.

But what I've come to understand is this:
it wasn't my body that betrayed me.

It was my detachment from it.

TORN HEART

The years I ignored its whispers, numbed its cries, silenced its wisdom.

The healing began not when I pushed harder,

but when I listened deeper.

When I let movement become medicine—not punishment.

Some days, that meant walking slowly around the block with my sons.
Some days, it meant stretching on the floor, tears pooling in the corners of my eyes.
And some days, it meant placing my hand over my heart and simply saying: "I'm still here."

Movement didn't fix me. It freed me.

It allowed emotion to move through me instead of getting stuck in me. It helped me process the things I couldn't yet speak aloud. The grief. The anger.
The rebirth. Because sometimes the body can hold what the heart isn't ready to unpack.

This is why I believe so deeply in movement—not just as a form of fitness, but as a sacred form of self-communication. When you M.O.V.E., you return to yourself.

You remember your aliveness.
You remember your power.
You remember that healing is never passive—it's an act of deep, embodied courage.

🌀 **Reader Reflection Prompt:**

When was the last time you listened to your body instead of judging it?

What does your body need right now—not to perform, not to prove—but to feel safe, strong, and seen?

Let it speak. Then move with love.

Listen to the Whisper—Why Your Body and Voice Matter

(*A sidebar from the Author*)

There's a voice inside you.
Not the loud, polished one you use in rooms where you feel safe…
but the quiet, instinctual one that lives deep in your belly.
That voice is your knowing.
And you were born with it.

For years, I ignored mine.
I overrode my body's signals.
I silenced the whispers because I thought being "fine" was safer than being *seen*.

But the truth is—your body knows before your mind does.
It knows when something isn't right.
It tightens. It aches. It trembles. It screams.

You don't need permission to trust that feeling.

You don't need credentials to speak up.
You don't need to be perfect or polite or "easy to work with" in order to be taken seriously.

You are allowed to advocate for your own care.
You are allowed to ask more questions.
You are allowed to say "This doesn't feel right"—and keep saying it until someone listens.

Whether it's a doctor's office, a relationship, a job, or a moment that seems small but doesn't sit right—
you are worthy of listening to your gut, honoring your body, and using your voice.

Let this be your reminder:
- You don't have to justify your intuition.
- You don't have to apologize for your sensitivity.
- You don't have to wait until you're falling apart to be taken seriously.

You are not too much.
You are not imagining it.
You are not wrong for needing more.

You are wise.
You are worthy.
And your body has been trying to tell you the truth all along.

Let This Be Your M.O.V.E.

You don't have to be unbreakable to rebuild. You don't need to wait for the perfect moment to begin again. You don't even need to know where you're going. You just need to be willing to move.

And not in the way the world always tells you—not hustle, not pressure, not perfection. But in this way: With courage. With choice. With love.

M.O.V.E. is more than my framework—it's my heart on paper. It's how I found my way back to myself. And it's what I offer to you now.

Take what resonates. Leave what doesn't. But know this: you're not alone. You never were.

You are allowed to begin again. You are allowed to heal at your own pace. And you are allowed to rise—softer, stronger, and more you than ever before.

So when life breaks you open, when the road curves unexpectedly, when the old ways no longer work...

Don't freeze.

Don't disappear.

M.O.V.E.

I'll be right here, cheering you on.

Before You Go—This Is Bigger Than One Diagnosis

Before we move into the final steps of this chapter,
there's something important I need to say.

This framework—this movement—wasn't born just from my SCAD diagnosis.
It was born from everything.

The eating disorder I hid behind gym mirrors.
The anxiety I masked with achievement.
The trauma I carried for years in silence.
The guilt of motherhood.
The unraveling of identity.
The loss of my body, my sport, my stability.

All of it shaped me.
All of it built this.

SCAD cracked me open—but the cracks were already there,
etched from a lifetime of holding it all together.

This wasn't the first time I had to start over.
But it *was* the first time I did it on my own terms—
with grace, with truth, with softness that didn't mean weakness.

So if you're reading this and thinking:
"But my story's different…"

Know this:

You don't need a diagnosis to be broken open.
You don't need a hospital wristband to justify your pain.
You don't need permission to begin again.

You are allowed to change your life at any point.
You are allowed to reclaim your strength—no matter where the fracture began.
Your story is enough.
And your healing is valid.

Putting M.O.V.E. Into Practice

You don't have to do it all today.
You don't need a perfect plan.
You just need one honest moment. One small choice.

Circle what you need most right now:

☐ **Manage:** What can I take control of—right here, right now?
☐ **Overcome:** What truth have I been avoiding that's ready to be seen?
☐ **Value:** What did today teach me—even if it was hard or quiet?
☐ **Evolve:** What part of me is ready to rise—even if I'm still afraid?

Now, write this down somewhere you'll see it:

"Today, I choose to _____, because I am worth it."

TORN HEART

Say it out loud.
Say it again if you need to.
Let it echo in your body.

Because this isn't about doing everything.
It's about doing the next thing—with courage, intention, and heart.

And if no one else listens, may you never stop listening to your body.
Let that be your power.

And now, before we move on, take a breath.
The next chapter isn't about steps or pillars.
It's about truths to hold when you forget your own.
A compass.
A soul-map.
The roar and the whisper that always lead you home.

CHAPTER 13

The M.O.V.E. Compass

A Soul Map Back to Yourself

"It's your road, and yours alone. Others may walk it with you, but no one can walk it for you."
— Rumi

Finding Your True North

The M.O.V.E. Compass is not a to-do list.
It's a lifeline.

These are the truths I held onto when I almost gave up.
The words I whispered when I thought I couldn't go on.
The declarations that kept me moving when stillness felt safer.

Some days they came out as a roar.
Other days as a whisper.
Both are powerful.
Both are yours.

Read them out loud.

Read them in silence.
Return to them as often as you need.

Because words transform.
And these words will hold you until you can hold yourself again.

✴ The Compass Points

I move because I am worthy.
I move even when I'm afraid.
I move toward myself, not away.
I manage what I can—and release what I can't.
I breathe when words won't come.
I overcome by choosing truth, not denial.
I value the pain because it shapes my power.
I evolve, even when I don't feel ready.
I rise, even in the ache.
I soften without shrinking.
I slow down—and still move forward.
I choose progress over perfection.
I trust the whispers more than the noise.
I let go with grace.
I begin again without apology.
I speak, even when my voice shakes.
I am not behind—I am becoming.
I remember who I am.
I M.O.V.E., because I was never meant to stay still.

Read this whenever you feel scattered or uncertain.

Come back when the days get loud.
Let these lines ground you, remind you:
You are the revolution.
You are the rise.
You are the reason your story still matters.

Each truth is a pulse, a breath, a step.
Together, they will carry you forward—
into the becoming that is already yours.

A Whisper for the Days You Forget

Some days you need a rallying cry. Other days, you need gentleness more than fire. These same truths, softened, are for the moments when your heart feels tender, when the mirror feels unfamiliar, when grief or doubt takes hold.

Read these slowly. Let them echo through your body.
You don't need to roar.
You only need to remember.
You are still here. And that is enough.

- I move because I am worthy.
- Even when I shake, I rise.
- I choose truth over silence.
- I lean into the wind, not away.
- I breathe when the words won't come.
- I walk through fear with open hands.
- I do not need to be perfect to be powerful.

- I let go, not because I'm weak, but because I'm ready.
- I start again, and again, and again.
- I trust what's blooming—even if I can't yet see it.
- I remember who I am.
- I M.O.V.E.—because becoming, even quietly, is still becoming.

☑ Ten Micro-Moves That Changed My Life

Here's what M.O.V.E. looked like when it was quiet, messy, and deeply human.

These aren't grand gestures. These are the sacred, small shifts that brought me back home to myself:

1. Sitting in stillness for 60 seconds—just breathing
2. Placing my hand over my heart and whispering, "I'm still here"
3. Choosing at least one nourishing meal a day—not perfect, just kind
4. Saying no to one thing that drained me
5. Repeating one M.O.V.E. mantra out loud, even when I didn't believe it yet
6. Walking outside and feeling the sun hit my face and the grass beneath my feet
7. Stretching on the floor with no plan, just feeling
8. Crying—without apology or explanation
9. Writing down one thing I was proud of, no matter how small
10. Naming one thing I was grateful for—even on the hard days
11. Texting someone *"thank you"* or *"I miss you"*—even if I didn't get a reply

These were the real wins. Not flashy. Not shareable. But holy. Start small. Start soft. But start.

What Three Words Describe Your M.O.V.E.?

You've just read my truths. You've seen what movement looks like—bold, soft, messy, sacred.

Now it's your turn.

When we're in transition—healing, evolving, rising—it helps to anchor ourselves in language that reflects who we are becoming. These words can guide your energy, shape your next steps, and define your impact.

Your three words are more than just adjectives.
They're a mirror.
A map.
A quiet declaration of who you are and what you're stepping into.

Let them guide your energy. Shape your next steps. Define your impact.

Tara's M.O.V.E. in Three Words:

1. **Transformational**—I don't just help people survive—I help them rise.
2. **Empowered**—My strength is in showing others their own.
3. **Purpose-Fueled**—Everything I do has heart behind it.

Now it's your turn.

Breathe for a moment. Drop into your body.

What three words describe your M.O.V.E.?
(Write them below—trust what rises.)

1. _____

2. _____

3. _____

Before You Go—Take This With You

You don't have to remember every word.
You don't have to hold it all at once.
You just need something to return to—when the day gets loud, when the ache returns.

Let these truths live where you need them most:
in your mirror, in your journal, whispered before sleep.

> And if you'd like a printable version of the compass, the whisper, and the reflection prompts, I created a free bundle for you at **www.tarabenoit.com/MOVE.**
>
> Keep it close. Let it guide you. And know you don't have to do this alone.

Let them remind you:
You don't have to be loud to be powerful.
You don't have to be perfect to be worthy.

TARA BENOIT

You don't have to do it all today.

But you do get to begin.

And I M.O.V.E.—not just to survive,
but to become.

PART FOUR

BECOMING

The Breaking Open Becomes The Becoming.
The Journey That Never Ends.
The Deepening Into Who We Are Meant To Be.

CHAPTER 14

When the Heart Ignites

*"Love and compassion are necessities, not luxuries.
Without them, humanity cannot survive."*
–Dalai Lama

The Flame That Followed the Fracture

Not long into the beginning of my recovery, I realized something powerful: To truly heal, I had to give back.

Helping others became a lifeline—not just for them, but for me.
I started reaching out to local heart health groups like the American Heart Association, eager to learn, to advocate, to connect. And what I learned broke my heart.

I discovered how under-researched women's cardiovascular health truly is—how many women are misdiagnosed, dismissed, or forgotten. I thought of my sons. Of their future partners. Of the daughters they might have one day. And I knew: I couldn't sit still. I had to do something.

I told Dr. T (a nickname I gave her, which she may not even fully know—like a superhero) that I wanted to help however I could. If there was anything I could do to support women with SCAD or raise awareness for women's heart health, I was in. All in.

Shortly after, I was contacted by MGH and asked if I'd be willing to share my story—to be featured on their website. I didn't even hesitate. That was a *hard yes.*

The article was beautifully written. Honest. Real. Hopeful.
And I felt deeply honored to share it—not for recognition, but to help other women feel seen. To remind them they weren't alone.
To begin again—not just as a survivor, but as a storyteller.

To this day, women still reach out to me because they saw that article and it gave them hope. Some message me from hospital beds, scared and searching, just like I once was. Their words remind me why I keep saying yes. Why I keep showing up. Because this isn't just a story I survived—
It's a story I'm called to share.

Then, a new moment and a door opened up that I didn't know I was ready for—one that led me to Dr. Nandita Scott. Like Dr. Tsiaras, she was another extraordinary woman cardiologist, with titles that spoke volumes and a presence that spoke even louder.

She welcomed me with warmth and purpose, and as we connected, something clicked. Dr Scott is wildly committed to helping women like me—women often overlooked in the world of heart disease. She didn't just see me as a patient or a story. She saw me as a voice—someone who could help reach others still in the dark.

Soon after, I was invited to speak at Heart & Vascular Design Day on a patient panel, standing beside two other heart survivors on the MGH stage. My hands trembled as I took the mic—not from weakness, but from the weight of what it meant to speak. In those moments, I had a full heart. This was my *why*. That was the moment I realized: I wasn't just healing... I was here to *help heal others*.

That one article had opened the door. But sharing my story on that stage—*that* was the moment the flame became the fire.

I spent months talking to and listening to other women, hearing their stories of heartbreak, loss, and survival. Some didn't have a voice yet. Others didn't know where to begin their healing. Many had no support system at all—just a compassionate doctor if they were lucky. Some were living in parts of the country without access to proper care. It devastated me. Because I knew how hard it had been for me... and I couldn't imagine walking this road with even fewer resources, fewer answers, or without someone in your corner.

These conversations broke my heart and fueled it at the same time. They reminded me why I couldn't turn away. Why I had to keep showing up. This wasn't just about awareness anymore—it was about honoring their pain with action. It was about being a voice, especially for those still finding theirs.

> 💔 **One in three women** will die from cardiovascular disease—making it the leading cause of death for women globally.
>
> 🩺 **Less than half of women** are even aware it's their greatest health threat.
>
> 🫀 Research still underrepresents women, and symptoms are often misdiagnosed, dismissed, or ignored.
>
> *(Source: American Heart Association)*

Behind every statistic is someone's mother, sister, daughter, or friend. Women like me. Women like the ones I love.

That's when I knew I couldn't look away. I had to speak up. I had to do something.

That is when I found the American Heart Association and Go Red for Women, which became powerful allies. I sought out local chapters, reached out to anyone I could, and started attending events, slowly getting involved.

Sharing my story, showing up, offering my heart—it all lit a spark in me. Advocacy was what filled my cup. Speaking up for women's heart health gave me a reason to rise each day. Sharing my story gave the pain a purpose. Slowly, I began to find the power in surrender—not as a weakness, but as a redirection. A rebirth.

And so, I said yes. To events, to connection, to anything that aligned with the new version of me. The version who wasn't afraid to be seen—even when she was still healing.

But the path forward wasn't straight. It twisted and curved, sometimes circling back into places I thought I'd already left behind.

Because I still had to navigate my heart—in every sense.

Podcasts, Besties, and the Birth of Purpose

Sometimes the people who save you don't wear scrubs or capes; they wear hoodies, hold coffee, and speak your soul's language without saying a word. Some of the people who saved me over the last couple of years weren't doctors or healers by trade—but they were soul surgeons just the same. They were my friends. My lifelines. My steady hands when mine were shaking.

They texted when I couldn't speak.
Called when I wanted to disappear.
Listened through the sobs, and never flinched at the silence.

They didn't need perfect words.
They just needed to be there.
And they were—again and again.

These are the women who knew what I needed before I did. Who could feel my unraveling through a single emoji. The ones who reminded me who I was when I forgot. They were the memory keepers, the light holders, the truth-tellers. And their love became part of my healing.

This kind of friendship? It's sacred.
Born not just from time, but from presence.
Not just from fun, but from fire.

Some I've known forever. Some came in like angels exactly when I needed them most. Each one arrived as part of the divine choreography that brought me back to life.

They didn't try to fix it.
They didn't rush my healing.
They just stood close—heart to heart—and whispered,
"You're not alone. I've got you."

And that was enough. More than enough.

For each of you reading this—
if you know this was you, please know this: *I will always hold a sacred place in my heart for you.*

During that first year, my mind often felt like a battlefield. I was trying to move forward, to reclaim some sense of normalcy, but the weight of everything I'd been through kept pulling me back—grief, fear, identity loss, all of it tangled together.

One afternoon, my soul sister bestie Brigette, "B," as I call her, called me just to check in. She always knows. Always. The kind of friend who doesn't wait for you to say you're not okay.

"T," she said softly, using the nickname only she does, "you have to listen to Ed Mylett's podcast. I know it will help you."

She didn't push. Just planted the seed. And that one seed—that small gesture—became something much bigger. A spark. A reminder. A thread of hope when I needed it most. B has always been that kind of anchor.

Her love is steady, intuitive, fierce in its softness.
And in that moment, she wasn't just giving me a podcast recommendation, she was giving me her heart. Her presence. Her belief in me when I couldn't feel it myself.

Some friendships come in like lightning. Ours has been the slow, steady burn of a sacred flame—a forever kind of love. Having met the day before 9/11, we always knew our friendship had a deep, special kind of love. And that day, it wasn't just a check-in. It was a turning point.

Believe it or not, I had never listened to a podcast before. But that first episode hit me like a ton of bricks. Ed featured people who had lived through life-altering experiences—people who didn't just survive, but grew from the wreckage. Their stories were raw, real, and full of resilience. They didn't sugarcoat the pain. They turned it into purpose.

It became a quiet ritual. Those morning doses of inspiration helped reframe my thinking and reconnect me to hope. Hearing others share their rock bottoms, their battles, and how they rose again gave me something to hold onto. It gave me a reason to get up, even when the simple act of getting my kids ready for school felt like climbing Everest. Those voices helped me remember I wasn't alone. And that maybe, just maybe, I could rise too.

Healing on My Terms

Although many heart and SCAD patients remain on medications for life, I made a quiet decision early on—that wouldn't be my path. Not out of pride. Not from pressure. But from deep personal intuition. I was determined to explore another way, and with the support of my care team, we worked toward that goal together—slowly, carefully, intentionally.

I truly believe the way I had cared for my body over the years—the discipline, the movement, the mindfulness—created a foundation that made it possible. But that's just *my* foundation.

Every patient is different. Every heart is different.

Some may need medication forever. Others, for a season. And neither is more right, stronger, or more healed than the other. What matters is that you feel safe. That you feel supported. That you honor your own nervous system and trust your timeline, not someone else's.

There is no prize for tapering off. No gold star for "doing it naturally." There is only your healing. Your safety. Your story.

I began the process gently. Bit by bit, I tapered off medications. I started layering in small rituals of healing—tiny anchors of structure woven into my days. Nothing dramatic. Just consistent, intentional choices. *Because I've learned that transformation rarely comes all at once.* It's built in the quiet, ordinary moments—the ones that slowly, faithfully, lead to something greater.

Every rep, every tear, every shaky step back into that space reminded me of this truth: healing doesn't always roar—sometimes it whispers. And strength? It's not in the weight you lift. It's in the courage to step into the unknown.

The Quiet Courage to Begin Again

There were days when I felt strong and lit up by purpose. And then there were days when I was run down, tired, sick… and my heart would ache. Not just emotionally—physically. A tightening, a heaviness, a whisper that said, "Slow down." I had to learn to live in this new body, with this new rhythm. It was humbling.

Listening to my body had always come naturally to me—I knew its rhythms, its whispers, its warning signs. I had built a career and a life rooted in physical awareness. But still, I pushed. Through pain. Through exhaustion. Through every limit I could find. That's how I had built success. That's how I had survived. I didn't ignore my body—I *drove* it. I overrode the signals not out of disconnection, but out of discipline, out of necessity.

And now? I had to unlearn that pattern. I had to shift from mastery to mercy. From pushing to pausing. From leading my body… to listening more deeply than ever before. I had to retrain my instincts—not to go harder, but to go softer. Not to ignore the signs, but to honor them.

It was one of the hardest things I've ever done.

But it's also what saved me.

Returning to hot yoga came with its own set of challenges. Once the woman at the front of the heated class, doing every pose past the point of holding, I now lay quietly on my mat near the door, where it was cooler, with a small fan I brought from home.

Sometimes, I simply rested there for a good portion of the class. I had an incredible yoga support system, and it helped me stay connected to my breath, my body, and my healing. I made the adjustments I needed to because of my heart—and over time, my practice became a companion in my recovery. Yes, it looked different. But so did I.

And through it all, my boys were watching.

They were watching how I responded to fear, to change, to uncertainty. Watching whether I stayed down or got back up. I knew I couldn't just tell them about resilience—I had to live it.

If I didn't show them what it meant to rise after life breaks you... who would?

So I kept going. Even when it was messy. Even when it hurt. I wanted them to see that you don't give up when life shifts under your feet—you adapt. You find new ways forward. You rest, and then you rise.

That was as important as any doctor's visit, any medication, any moment of strength I could muster.

As part of that healing, I also began opening up to my boys more about what had happened—what SCAD was, how it changed me, and why I was working so hard to be better. They came to hear me speak, and I saw it settle in their hearts. They were proud of me, and that made me even prouder.

We became a team. As a family, we wore matching SCAD T-shirts I had made for a 2024 SCAD Synopsis event at Mass General Hospital and the Boston AHA Walk. They still wear them, proudly.

Even as I write this book, I was recently "drafted" by Tedy Bruschi and Damar Hamlin through Abbott's HeartMates Program for the 2025 HeartMates Draft. Fellow heart survivors themselves, I was blown away by their will and drive to make a difference. We got to meet and even talk on a call. My boys—huge football fans—were beyond excited.

I share this not to impress, but to express something deeper: the importance of serving and helping others. Because when you do that—when you show up, heart first—it doesn't matter who you are. We all become one.

Movement, Again—But Different

What began years earlier as painful steps back into the gym had become something steadier, more sacred. I had kept going, slowly, imperfectly, until one day I realized: it wasn't about reclaiming who I was, but honoring who I'd become.

I walk into the gym now with something I never had before—
Peace. Not pressure. Not punishment. Just presence.

I give myself grace. I feel what I'm doing. I listen to her—my body—instead of beating her up. And the more I fall into this rhythm of self-respect, the better I feel. Not just in my skin… but in my *spirit*.

TORN HEART

I've lived on both ends of the spectrum.
I've been underweight. I've been over.
I've been gripped by eating disorders.
I've been curled up in depression, in anxiety, in grief, in post-heart attack exhaustion.

And my number one takeaway?

If you don't have your health, you have nothing.

Movement has always been my medicine. It always will be.
But it looks different now. And that's okay.

Because we're not meant to stay the same forever.
We're meant to *shift*. To *shed*. To *evolve*.
And learning to move with your life—instead of against it—is one of the most sacred forms of self-acceptance I've ever known.

These days, I watch other women at the gym—all ages, all walks of life—and I feel something deep, soul-level. Pride. Joy. Honor.

There's something holy about watching a woman choose herself.
I will always feel most myself in places where bodies move, hearts open, and strength is not just seen—but *felt*.

Well… that and the ocean.
Because sometimes, the tide teaches us just as much as the barbell.

When Faith Finds You Again

Now came something I didn't expect at all. After losing my faith in God as a young adult, my life had really taken on a spiritual shape—but not a religious one. I had always considered myself someone with a spiritual connection, but not bound by traditional faith.

Then, during my healing, something shifted. One of Ed's podcast episodes led me down a new path—or maybe it was an old one resurfacing. That episode featured Pastor Steven Furtick, and his words stirred something I didn't know was still inside me. Ed, I know one day we will meet, and I will get to tell you how you were a part of my healing and how it helped me start this legacy I am called to.

I started listening to Pastor Steven's YouTube sermons, and they spoke in ways that truly resonated. His words reached into the spaces that had long been closed off.

I was surprised—and honestly, I didn't tell anyone. Not because I was ashamed, but because I wasn't sure where this part of me fit anymore.

But then I listened to another sermon. And another. And slowly, something inside me began to stir. A flicker of faith that had been absent for decades quietly crept back into my body… into my heart.

I have chills even writing this now. My faith—once buried—was waking up. And today, it's bigger and bolder than ever. Things I never would've done before the heart attack. I never had time. But the truth is, time is all we *do* have. When you realize that, you begin to make space for what truly matters. I'm still discovering who I am in this new light—still softening, still strengthening. Because becoming isn't a moment. It's a lifetime.

I didn't just survive that year. I was remade by it. Piece by piece, I became someone softer and stronger. Someone who listens, who leads, who lifts. And maybe most importantly—someone who believes. In love. In purpose. In faith. In something greater. This was no longer just recovery. It was a rebirth.

And as I kept showing up—to the new events, to the speaking stage, to my own unfolding—something new began to stir.

Not a return to who I was…

But the quiet creation of who I was becoming.

A New Platform, A New Pulse

Somewhere along this road—between the quiet yoga mat moments and the echoes of women's stories I couldn't forget—a seed began to stir in me. I realized I wasn't just healing… I was *building*.

At 48, I'm creating something new.
Not because I have all the answers, but because I finally asked the right question: **What if the next chapter of your life isn't about proving your worth—but *sharing* it?**

So I'm building a platform—a sacred space where women can come home to themselves.
A place where purpose meets healing.
Where personal development, women's health, advocacy, and resilience all find a seat at the table.

This isn't a pivot. It's a *becoming*.

And you don't have to be 25 or 30 or even 40 to begin again.
You just have to be ready.
Ready to rise from what broke you and build from the bones of your truth.

Because the truth is—I don't want to just speak about survival anymore.
I want to help others live.
Fully. Bravely. Now.

♡ From My Heart to Yours

Maybe you're standing in the wreckage of a life that once made sense. Maybe you're holding the pieces of a dream that doesn't fit anymore. If that's where you are, know this: the pieces can still become something beautiful.

There is no shame in letting go of something that once defined you—especially when it no longer honors who you are becoming.

You don't have to know exactly where you're going to take the first step. You just have to trust that your healing, your heartbreak, and your hope are not random—they are all part of your becoming.

If you're a parent, like me, you know the eyes that watch you aren't just looking—they're *learning*. And one of the most powerful lessons we can ever teach our children is this:
We don't stay down.
We rise.
We find new ways.
Even when it's hard. *Especially* when it's hard.

Let the pain shape you, not break you.

You are not behind. You are right on time.

Let's keep moving—together.

CHAPTER 15

The Truth About Transformation

"You can't go back and change the beginning, but you can start where you are and change the ending."
–C.S. Lewis

Mental Health, Money & the Weight We Don't Talk About

This isn't the chapter I wanted to write.

It's the one I had to. They say healing is a journey—but they don't always say how raw the road can get when you're still on it.

I thought the hardest part was over. The diagnosis, the hospital, the slow climb back into my body.

But no one warns you about the after.

No one tells you that sometimes, the real storm comes after the spark—when the world sees you as a survivor, a light, a voice… But inside, you're still standing in the rubble.

This chapter isn't past-tense. I'm still in it. There are days I cry on the bathroom floor—not because I'm broken, but because the weight of being

strong has worn me thin. Sometimes I look at my finances and remember where I was just a few years ago—
how steady things felt, how secure. And then I think about how one event—one moment—can reroute your entire life. The trajectory shifts. What was once stable becomes uncertain.
And suddenly, you're rebuilding everything you thought would never break.

I had worked so hard for so long—always moving, always building, always carrying the next thing forward.
So when life forced me to slow down, it didn't just affect my heart.
It cracked open everything: my rhythm, my identity, my finances, my sense of safety.

I wasn't just healing from a physical rupture; I was trying to rebuild a life from the inside out.

That meant facing hard truths: Despite the passion I had for this new path, I was walking away from something already built,
something that had once held me—and my family—steady.

I was chasing purpose, impact, changing lives—and praying that chasing what mattered wouldn't cost me everything else.

I was deeply called to serve—to write, to speak, to lead—
but I was also deeply scared of how uncertain it all felt.

And yet, in the quiet, I still hear a whisper:
"Keep going."

Not because it's easy, but because I've come this far.

Because I know too much now to go back.
Because maybe this isn't falling apart. Maybe this is the shape of rising.

Despite the uneasiness of all of it, I'm writing this anyway—for you.
For the woman holding it all together with whispered prayers and quiet breakdowns.
For the leader who doesn't know how to say, "I'm not okay."
For the mother, the daughter, the friend who shows up for everyone else while feeling like she's disappearing inside herself.

Maybe the bravest thing I've done this year…
is writing this chapter,
while still in the storm.

It's a strange in-between.

To feel full of light and still feel the darkness tug at your ankles.
To be awake in your spirit, but exhausted in your mind.
And maybe that's the part no one talks about—the *bothness* of it all.

But I'm here to tell you:
You can hold both.
You can walk through this fog and still be moving forward.
You can cry and still be healing.
You can question and still have purpose.
This moment—this very one—doesn't disqualify you from the joy that's still coming.

I feel better than I have in a long time—
but the weight of everything else?
It's still heavy.

TORN HEART

The kind of heavy that aches in your bones.

How do you get past that place?

Maybe you don't "get past" it.
Maybe you walk with it.
Maybe you learn to breathe inside it.

If you're in that place right now—
I see you.
You're not doing it wrong.
You're just becoming.

This isn't the end of your story.
It's the middle.
And you're allowed to take a breath here—
then rise when you're ready.

CHAPTER 16

A Love Letter to the Reader

"Beauty begins the moment you decide to be yourself."
–Coco Chanel

Dear beautiful soul,

If you've made it this far, I want to say something to you—not as the author, not as the woman who lived this story, but as someone who deeply understands what it means to fall apart and try again.

Thank you for walking beside me—for listening, for feeling, for letting parts of my journey echo in your own. That's what sharing does. It braids us together. It reminds us we're never really alone.

This book isn't just about my healing. It's about *yours*, too. It's about showing you that even the most broken seasons can become sacred. That even the messiest, most uncertain chapters can be rewritten.

If you saw yourself in these pages—in the panic, the pain, the rising—I want you to hold that gently. Let it be proof that your story matters. That your healing is valid. That your becoming is already in motion.

You don't have to have it all figured out. You don't have to be finished to be free. You just have to be willing to begin.

I wrote this book from my heart, and I hand it to you, heart to heart. May it meet you right where you are and gently guide you to where you're meant to go.

With love,
Tara 🩶

CHAPTER 17

This Is Your Permission Slip

"Only do what your heart tells you."
–Princess Diana

Let me ask you something I had to ask myself: Are you walking around just existing… or are you answering the call you feel deep in your bones?

That whisper of more—more purpose, more joy, more alignment. That sacred nudge that says, "You were made for something greater."

I know what it's like to shrink. To go through the motions. To stay small because survival felt like the only option. Perhaps you are battling in silence—and from the outside, no one knows. But I see you.

Maybe you're living with a condition you don't fully understand. Maybe the words on your medical chart feel more like question marks than answers. I know what it's like to try and wrap your mind around something invisible, unpredictable—something that could happen again. To live with uncertainty tucked behind every heartbeat, every breath. But still, you rise.

This? This chapter in your life isn't just about getting through. It's about coming alive.

You were never meant to just exist. You were meant to live boldly, fully, honestly—and beautifully out loud.

So here's your permission slip: To dream. To shift. To grow into the vision that's been tugging at your spirit.

I used to think permission had to come from someone else—a doctor, a boss, a spouse, a sign from the universe. But after my heart attack, everything changed. I realized no one was coming to save me. So I gave myself permission to begin.

To write this book. To share my story. To rest. To speak. To rise. Even when I was scared. Especially when I was scared.

Now I want you to do the same. Not because it's easy. But because you're worth it.

You are capable of what you manifest. You are allowed to change everything. You are allowed to want more—and get it.

This is your moment. Your breath. Your breakthrough.

I'll be right here, cheering you on as you say yes to the next brave chapter of your becoming.

CHAPTER 18

Uncontrollably in Control

"Ruin is a gift. Ruin is the road to transformation."
–Elizabeth Gilbert, Eat, Pray, Love

✈ From Panic to Peace

It's spring 2025, and I am just weeks away from the second anniversary of my SCAD heart attack, and I'm getting ready to fly solo. I am sitting in the front row of a JetBlue airplane headed to Dallas, Texas—and I am alone. Me, myself, and I. Just one year ago, this would have been unthinkable.

If you'd asked me five or ten years ago if I would ever fly alone, I would've laughed. Loud. I might've bet a million dollars against it.

I've always been a growth-minded woman. But even the most driven, optimistic people carry their shadows. For me, that shadow was *control*. Or more accurately, fear of losing it.

For decades, I lived with debilitating panic disorder. From the outside, I looked composed: high-achieving, motivated, well-dressed, always "on."

But inside? It was chaos. Being in closed spaces triggered full-body terror—my nervous system hijacked by fear, spiraling into fight or flight. I was a high-functioning, overachieving woman who lived with this silently for years—juggling success on the outside while constantly managing crisis on the inside.

For many years, I avoided malls, concerts, crowded places—anything that might trap me without a quick exit or sense of control. If I went, it was with an escape route memorized.

Flying? Out of the question. Sure, I'd traveled once or twice a year before having kids, but every trip came with anxiety and terror. A locked metal box 30,000 feet in the air—no exits, no escape. Just trust. Just surrender. That was too much for me. I loved the *idea* of travel. But the reality felt like torture.

Still, there was a whisper in me. A longing for *more*. For life beyond the fear. My mother—my best friend—gave me my love of adventure. She raised me to believe the world was meant to be explored, to chase joy, and to find courage in the unknown. That spirit stayed with me. And over time, even in the middle of my fear, that belief started to rise inside me too.

First, I flew with family. Always hard. I'd worry for hours before takeoff, manage symptoms in silence, and watch others laugh or sleep with envy. *How are they so calm?* I wondered. *Why can't I be like that?*

Then came motherhood. And with it, something shifted. I wanted to be brave—not just for me, but for my boys. I wanted them to see a woman who rose. Who *showed up*.

Still, I never flew alone. Until now.

So how did I get from panic to peace? One word: **transformation.**

But not the overnight kind. This transformation was slow, tender, and often invisible to others. It came from years of therapy, inner work, and uncomfortable self-awareness. It came from learning to breathe through fear instead of running from it. From stretching my tolerance, from honoring small wins, from failing and trying again.

It came from showing up even when I was trembling and realizing that fear didn't mean I was broken. It meant I was human. And that I could still move forward anyway.

This transformation wasn't accidental. It was born from thousands of tiny, intentional choices—the kind most people never see. I practiced yoga for over twenty-five years, often just to feel my breath again. I moved my body regularly—not to punish it, but to partner with it. From lifting weights to long walks, from cycling to stretching, I learned that movement could be medicine. I said no when it would've been easier to say yes. I spent my entire adult life committed to body and mind healing through massage therapy, movement, and other sacred practices.

Since I was 21, I have returned to the massage table again and again—in moments of stress, seasons of strength, and stages of surrender. For all those years, my massage therapist, Laura, has been by my side—now also one of my closest friends. She became part of my rebirth. Her hands helped remind my body that it was still here. Still safe. Still mine. With her, it had always been this way—her touch more than technique, her presence more than practice. She didn't just care for my body; she cared for my healing, reminding me that my body could be a safe place to live, again and always.

I chose silence when the world demanded noise. I prioritized my health—fiercely. That meant full nights of sleep, movement over punishment, nutrition that nourished rather than numbed. It meant boundaries. It meant tuning in instead of checking out. My healing was a lifestyle long before it was a breakthrough.

This wasn't just about flying. It was about shedding old fear, rewiring my nervous system, and trusting that I was safe in *myself*. I was headed to an event to meet my mentor and coach, Amberly Lago, and other heart-led women. And for the first time, I didn't feel the weight of fear. I felt the lightness of freedom.

Healing is never linear. But sometimes, you wake up and realize: you're doing the very thing you used to run from. And you're not afraid.

This was one of those moments. It wasn't quiet—it was loud, bold, and electrifying. It felt like fireworks in my chest (the good kind), like the earth finally shifting beneath my feet. Not just an arrival in Dallas… but in my own becoming.

I can say with full certainty that this was a massive turning point in my life. It felt like everything I had worked toward—every quiet choice, every boundary I held, every moment I chose my breath over my fear—had brought me to this seat, on this plane, in this moment.

Maybe as you read this, you're thinking of something in your own life that's kept you bound—something you've lived with, hidden, or feared.

Maybe it's not flying for you. Maybe it's speaking your truth. Leaving a job. Ending a relationship. Saying yes to yourself for the first time.

Whatever it is… I want you to know: you're not alone. And you're not stuck.

This flight wasn't just a trip. It was a breakthrough. The catalyst that cracked it all open. I have never felt freer in my entire life. Ever.

May you find your own seat, your own sky, your own moment when fear finally gives way to freedom.

♡ From My Heart to Yours

Maybe your fear doesn't look like mine. Maybe it's not a plane, or a panic attack, or a moment of frozen breath. Maybe it's something quieter—a decision you haven't made, a dream you've buried, a life you've delayed.

But I want you to know this: your version of freedom is still possible.

Your healing may not come all at once. It might arrive in tiny moments—in the choice to get up, to try again, to say "not this time" when fear comes knocking.

You don't have to be fearless to be free. You just have to be willing to believe that change is possible—even for you.

You're not broken. You're becoming.

And this moment? It might be your seat on the plane.

I believe in your rise. I'm cheering for you. And I'm so honored to walk beside you—story to story, breath by breath, and heart to heart.

CHAPTER 19

Comfort Zones—The Edge of Becoming

"Just when the caterpillar thought the world was over, it became a butterfly."
—Proverb

Tiny Shifts, Tremendous Transformation

I often wonder if people realize just how much their lives could change—beautifully, radically—with a single decision.

Seems simple, doesn't it?

But that one decision often sits just outside the bounds of comfort—beyond the routines, the roles, the reasons we whisper to ourselves late at night.

I've had to push myself, again and again, past the familiar. I've stood at the edge of what I knew, trembling, aching, uncertain—hoping that on the other side lived a version of me I hadn't met yet. A version shaped by growth. By truth. By transformation.

And let me tell you: she was always worth it.

But I didn't always leap. Sometimes, I stayed. Stayed in the familiar. Stayed in the patterns. Stayed in the silence. Because the pain of change felt too big… too heavy… too unknown to carry.

Have you ever been there? Wanting something so deeply it lived in your bones—and yet, the leap felt just out of reach?

Let me ask you this:

What if taking that step—any step—opened a door to the very life you've been aching for?

What if the dream in your heart isn't random… but a roadmap?

What if you're closer than you think?

Because, my beautiful friend, you are.

We've talked about leaps, but let me remind you of this: it's not always the giant ones that change our lives… it's not always the giant leaps that change our lives. More often, it's the small, brave decisions—the tiny shifts—made again and again, that quietly reshape everything. One breath. One choice. One step. These become the building blocks of transformation. And as you take them, know this: I am here, walking beside you.

The life you long for—aligned, awake, alive—is possible. It's not for "other people." It's for you.

Right now. Right here.

Exactly as you are.

I won't tell you it's easy. Growth rarely is.

But I will tell you this: it's worth it.

The dark seasons. The cracked-open moments. The questions without answers.

They shape you. Refine you.

They ready you for your rise.

And I want to be honest with you—*I'm still on this journey too*. I'm still learning, still healing, still choosing to grow every single day.

There is no final destination, no perfect arrival. But there *is* a place more beautiful than I ever imagined—one rooted in love, peace, and purpose.

You are the butterfly in the cocoon—still, quiet, unseen. But strength is building. Wings are forming. And one day soon, you'll feel it:

That holy ache to fly.

And when you do?

The world will be ready.

And so will **you**.

Epilogue

"Be faithful in small things because it is in them that your strength lies."
–Mother Teresa

Forever Rising Higher

Life, healing, and becoming yourself are lifelong processes.

I used to think I was working so hard to get to one perfect place.
A finish line. A summit. A version of me that felt finally whole.

But through the tearing and rebuilding of my heart—literally and spiritually—I've realized we're never meant to arrive and stay there.
We're meant to evolve.
To stretch.
To shed.
To rise, fall, and rise again.

You get hurt. I get hurt.
We ache.
We heal.
We learn.
We remember how to belong to ourselves.

TORN HEART

There is no straight line, only a path lit by the truth we're brave enough to follow.

I've always felt a deep pull toward those who've lived through trauma. Even as a child, I could feel their ache. Their longing. Their quiet strength. It both scared and comforted me—as if I knew somehow I would walk that path one day too.

And now, I do—with a steadiness I didn't know I had.

I've learned to find joy in small, sacred ways:
The way the sunlight hits the trees.
The blue in the sky when the clouds finally break.
The ordinary magic of still being here.

Even now, I live with a condition that could return without warning.
I feel it sometimes—the awareness of my own heart, the echo of what tore through me.
But I no longer let it steal my peace.
I choose presence.
I choose now.
I choose to live like I've never lived before.

Strength, I've learned, is not in pretending you're fine.
It's in honoring the ache and still finding your breath.
Still choosing beauty. Still showing up.
Still learning how to love like never before.

We are never trapped. Not truly.
We are not made of cement—*we are water*.
We rise. We reshape. We become.

So I leave you here, not with an ending,
but with an invitation.

To return to the truth of who you are.
To unearth the parts of you buried beneath the wreckage.
To speak the thing you've been too scared to say.
To reclaim what the world tried to take.
To rise as you are, not as you were.

You are allowed to let go of the story that kept you small.
You are allowed to shed what no longer fits.
You are allowed to live differently now.
You are allowed to love like never before.

Because you are not broken.
You are being reborn.

Again and again—with every breath that says,
Stay. You have more to live for.

And if you listen closely—
in the quiet between heartbeats—
you might catch the whisper of something unfinished,
the echo of something only you say in your dreams.

Somewhere in the stillness between the waves and the wind,
a mountain still shifts.

You are rising.
You are becoming.
And the world has only just begun to feel your light.

I believe in you. I always will.

With all my heart,
Tara 🖤

Inspiring Hope. Moving Hearts. Rising Still.

Afterword

Doctors Who Walked Beside Me

SCAD and Hope for the Future

I've shared my heart with you. Now I want to close by sharing theirs—the doctors who cared for me after SCAD, when I needed both expertise and compassion. Dr. Sarah Tsiaras and Dr. Nandita Scott not only treated my heart, they reminded me it was still possible to live fully with it. Their wisdom and vision for the future of SCAD care offer an inspiring final word—not just for me, but for every woman who has ever felt unseen, dismissed, or afraid.

So I will let their voices speak here. What follows are not my words, but theirs—the words of the doctors who walked beside me, sharing their wisdom, their perspective, and their hope…

Socrates' observation that *"you don't know what you don't know"* aptly describes the historical state of knowledge regarding SCAD diagnosis and treatment. Years ago, during our cardiology training, SCAD was rarely even considered—even in patients presenting with cardiac symptoms whose angiograms appeared normal.

Ironically, years later, we would find ourselves in a program of experts dedicated to the care, education, and research of this very condition. This evolution underscores a broader reality: heart conditions that predominantly affect women have been underrecognized.

For decades, a pervasive misconception persisted that cardiovascular disease was not a major concern for women. It was not until 1993 that the NIH mandated inclusion of women in federally funded clinical research.

Nearly twenty years later, in 2012, the FDA began requiring sex-specific analyses in the review of drugs, biologics, and medical devices. This was followed in 2014 by an NIH policy recommending balanced representation of male and female cells and animals in preclinical studies. The consequences of this long-standing exclusion have been profound: cardiovascular research in women has lagged significantly behind that in men.

Research into spontaneous coronary artery dissection (SCAD) has followed a familiar pattern—growing steadily, yet still lagging behind the robust evidence base that informs care for plaque-mediated heart attacks. It is therefore no surprise that SCAD remains frequently unrecognized, its treatment approaches inconsistent, and lifestyle counseling for affected patients uneven.

Encouragingly, the past decade has brought meaningful change. National awareness campaigns, dedicated women's heart health programs, and an expansion of SCAD-focused research have driven real improvements in care and outcomes. Equally important, the voices of SCAD survivors have played a pivotal role in raising awareness and propelling the field forward.

Tara first came to our Women's Heart Health Program in July 2023, just two months after her SCAD diagnosis. She was discouraged and feeling down by the sudden life changes brought on by SCAD, and the accompanying exercise restrictions had left her feeling hopeless. Tearful and still in pain, she shared her story with us. Despite her despair, we believed she could recover and live fully after SCAD.

At the Mass General Brigham Women's Heart Health Program, we have had the privilege of guiding hundreds of SCAD survivors through this journey. While the road to recovery varies in scope and length, we have seen patients return to vibrant and meaningful lives.

What we could not yet know was how profoundly Tara's life—and her influence—would evolve, particularly in her role as a passionate patient advocate. Patients like Tara inspired us to launch a Sports SCAD program within the broader Women's Heart Health Program at MGB. Exercise is essential for both physical and mental health—particularly for those with heart disease—and through this initiative, we aim to show that exercise after SCAD can be safe when tailored to each patient's fitness level.

Still, much work remains. We face numerous unanswered questions about the diagnosis, treatment, and long-term management of SCAD. How can we identify those at risk before an event occurs? How do we prevent recurrence and determine who is at the highest risk for another event? Can we better understand which individuals can safely pursue pregnancy after SCAD? How should we approach hormone management—whether contraception, menopausal hormone therapy, or other uses? And, as highlighted by Tara's story, what type and amount of exercise can be safely recommended?

Our vision for the future is that every patient who presents with a cardiac event in the absence of plaque will have SCAD included in the differential diagnosis. Once diagnosed, care will follow evidence-based protocols that guide decisions about when to intervene, which medications are most effective in preventing recurrence, and how best to counsel patients on pregnancy, hormone use, and maintaining an active lifestyle. With continued research, clinical innovation, and the courage of survivors like Tara, we can ensure that "you don't know what you don't know" no longer applies to SCAD.

This book contributes to the growing effort to raise awareness about SCAD and honors the lived experiences of patients whose resilience and advocacy have propelled progress. I hope that Tara's story brings hope to readers—whether they are SCAD survivors or loved ones of survivors—showing that there is a way forward, and that people like Tara are living proof.

– Dr. Sarah V. Tsiaras
Medical Director, Mass General Brigham Heart Center, Waltham, MA
Mass General Brigham Healthcare Center, Waltham

– Dr. Nandita S. Scott
Director, Mass General Brigham Women's Heart Health Program
Director of Cardiovascular Medicine, Massachusetts General Hospital
Assistant Professor of Medicine, Harvard Medical School

Beyond The Story

What Waits Beyond the Last Page

The final chapter may have closed, but your journey doesn't end here. What follows is meant to extend the story you've just walked through—offering truths, tools, and reminders to carry with you as you step into your own becoming.

You've walked with me through my story—**now I want to walk with you as you step into your own.**

Here you'll find reflections on living with SCAD, an invitation to what the world needs from you, closing messages for your heart, and resources to guide your next steps.

My hope is that this part of the book feels less like an ending and more like a hand extended—reminding you that healing, purpose, and connection continue beyond the story.

SCAD – The Beat That Remains

A Survivor's Voice for Us All

You don't expect your heart to tear when you're healthy.
You don't expect to be dismissed when you're scared.
But for so many women, that's exactly what happens.

We say we're in pain, and they call it anxiety.
We whisper that something's wrong, and they tell us we're fine.

Living with SCAD means learning a new normal.
It's waking up every day with a heart that's been torn open—
and still finding the courage to listen to it.

This is about more than recovery.
This is about women being heard.
It's time the world listened.

SCAD is always with me.
Not just the day it happened,
but in the quiet that follows.
When emotions rise,
my heart aches—
sometimes so much I have to stop.
To rest.

TORN HEART

It's almost like a third child.
Always there—reminding me, guiding me,
not letting me push when I want to.
It's grounded me in ways I never thought I could be.
It watches over me—
demanding presence, refusing to be ignored.

I've had to let go of being angry.
Only then could I step into purpose.
Into light.

None of this has been easy.
Every SCAD story is different.
Every survivor walks through it in her own rhythm,
her own pain,
her own timing.

This is just mine.
And my hope is that by sharing my voice—
by letting you see *me*—
the world might begin to see *you*, too.

I survived the tear in my heart.
But survival was only the beginning.
SCAD lingers in the aftermath—
in the quiet fears that surface,
in the skipped beat that makes you pause,
in the what if that hums beneath a sunny day.

SCAD changed me—
it didn't just tear my heart,
it tore through every part of my life.
It stripped away everything I thought I was:
strong, in control, untouchable.

But it gave me something too.
A softness I never allowed myself.
A strength I can't measure in miles or muscle.
A voice I no longer quiet.

I live with SCAD—
and I live fully.
Not in spite of the break.

But because of what it showed me:
That survival is not the end.
It's a beginning.
The opening.
The doorway **into your heart.**
Step through—
and you may be astonished
by the strength, the light,
and the life waiting there.

What the World Needs Now

Your Voice. Your Truth. Our Future.

What the world needs now isn't more noise.
It's more *honesty*.

Not perfection—but showing up as you are.
Speaking, even when your voice shakes.
Saying, *"This is my truth. This is what I've lived. And I'm still here."*

There is power in being raw.
There is freedom in being real.
And there is no greater rebellion than using your voice—fully, freely, fiercely.
Because when you silence yourself, you dim the person you were born to become.

When you hide your light, the world loses something only *you* can give.
Your presence becomes quieter. Your magic, more muted.
You shrink to make others comfortable—
but the price is your wholeness.

We tell our children: *"Speak up if someone hurts you."*
But somewhere along the road to adulthood, we stop giving ourselves that same permission.

TORN HEART

It's time we take it back.

What the world needs now are people who are no longer willing to betray their truth.
Who understand that being sensitive isn't a weakness, and softness isn't surrender.
People brave enough to rise, not for applause—but for alignment.

To walk their path.
To live their purpose.
To lead from the place where soul and story meet.

Because the world doesn't just need more voices.
It needs *yours*.

And when you rise, you light the way for the rest of us.

Now go.
Speak.
Shine.

The world is waiting.
I'm waiting too.

I See You

A Final Note and Invitation

If you're reading this, I want to thank you—not just for turning the pages, but for meeting me here with an open heart.

Writing this book was the most vulnerable I've ever felt.
I've shared things I once kept buried so deep I barely admitted them to myself.
It asked me to stand inside the cracks, to speak from the scar, to own the stories I once ran from.

But I did it—for me, and for you.

Because I believe stories heal.
And if even one line in these pages helped you feel seen… then it was worth every trembling word.

Maybe you saw pieces of yourself in this story—the strong one who kept going, the one who never felt quite "sick enough" or "healed enough," the one who's still learning to trust her voice, her body, her instincts.

Maybe you've been dismissed. Maybe you've carried pain in silence. Maybe you've built a life while feeling like parts of you were still buried beneath it.

TORN HEART

Whatever brought you here, I want you to know something:

You are not alone.
You are not broken.
You are not behind.

You are becoming. And you're already brave for being here.

If you've ever felt like you were meant for more—it's because you are.
If something inside you has whispered, *There's more to me than this...*
If you've dreamed of a life that feels freer, fuller, more aligned with your soul—
That's not a dream to dismiss—that's a truth to return to.

You don't have to wait until you're "ready."
You don't have to wait until you feel fixed.
You don't need permission.

You are capable. You are worthy.
You are already enough.

The path to healing curves, doubles back, and wanders. And sometimes, the greatest form of leadership is surviving and choosing to speak.
It looks like standing back up. Speaking up. Or whispering the truth you've never said out loud—even if it shakes.

You don't need permission to take your next step.
You only need one thing: to believe that your voice matters.

You've lived through so much.
Now it's time to live *from* it—with purpose.

Allowing yourself to believe—truly believe—that you are worthy and deserving of the life you always wanted…
is the key to setting yourself free.

Your voice is power.
It can break invisible chains you didn't even realize you had locked around yourself.

It is never too late.
There is never a perfect moment.
Time is precious. And this is your life.

You have one body, one soul, one wild and sacred chance to live fully.

So own it.
Take action.
Be bold.

**Cry. Scream. Love. Smile. Jump. Laugh. Sparkle. Dance.
Be silly. Be soft. Be loud. Be you.**

Your Next Step

Share this book with someone who needs to feel seen.
Start a conversation.
Book that appointment.
Speak your story.
Take one brave breath—and keep moving.
The world needs your voice.
And you, my beautiful fighter,
were born to rise.

What rising might look like:

- Saying the thing you've never said aloud
- Asking for help—and letting yourself receive it
- Reaching out to someone who gets it
- Resting, because your healing matters
- Writing your truth down, even if it stays just for you (for now)
- Making that first move—toward your body, your purpose, your peace

This is not about having it all figured out.
It's about finding the courage to begin again, with honesty and heart.

You're not broken.
You're becoming.

Heart Health Fact Sheet

What Every Woman Should Know

Cardiovascular disease remains the leading health threat for women—yet it is underdiagnosed, underresearched, and often misunderstood. These facts provide essential insight into why awareness and advocacy matter so deeply:

- Cardiovascular disease (CVD) is the leading cause of death for women in the U.S., accounting for one in every three female deaths.
    - Source: American Heart Association (AHA)

- SCAD (spontaneous coronary artery dissection) is a leading cause of heart attacks in women under 50—especially in healthy, active women with no traditional risk factors.
    - Source: Mayo Clinic/AHA/SCAD Alliance

- Women are 50% more likely than men to be misdiagnosed after a heart attack.
    - Source: Journal of the American Heart Association (JAHA)

- Only 38% of women recognize that heart disease is their greatest health threat.
    - Source: American Heart Association 2021 Awareness Study

- 80% of women miss the early signs of a heart attack because we're taught to push through the pain.
    - Source: Cleveland Clinic Women's Heart Health Study

- Emotional trauma can double a woman's risk of heart disease, and no one's talking about it.
    - Source: Harvard Women's Health Watch

- Chronic stress is a silent contributor to heart disease in women—especially caretakers, mothers, and high performers.
    - Source: Johns Hopkins Medicine

- Just 12% of practicing cardiologists are women, contributing to gender disparities in care.
    - Source: American College of Cardiology (ACC)

- Most cardiac rehab programs were originally designed around the needs of male patients and still lack gender-specific protocols.
    - Source: *Journal of Cardiopulmonary Rehabilitation and Prevention*

- Cardiovascular disease is the leading cause of maternal mortality in the United States.
    - Source: Centers for Disease Control and Prevention (CDC)

- Black women face a disproportionate risk—they are more likely to develop heart disease, experience pregnancy-related cardiac complications, and receive delayed or inadequate treatment.
    - Source: American Heart Association Scientific Statements/CDC

Why This Matters

These aren't just numbers. They're mothers, sisters, daughters, and friends.

They represent women walking through life unaware that the greatest threat to their health is hiding in plain sight. They represent women like me. Women like you.

This is us.

Sharing these truths isn't just about raising awareness—
It's about saving lives.
It's about changing the story.

One conversation. One heart. One woman at a time.

Let this be your reminder:
Your heart matters.
Your story matters.

And knowledge is power.

Then take a breath.
Place your hand over your heart.
And remember—you are not alone in this.

> Want to keep these heart health truths close—and share them with someone you love?
>
> Download the full Heart Health Companion Guide at:
>
> **www.tarabenoit.com/hearttruths**

Resources for Healing and Hope

Trusted Places for Care and Connection

If you're reading this and carrying something too heavy, too hidden, or too long-ignored, please hear this:

You are not alone. There are safe places to turn, real people who want to help, and tools that can meet you exactly where you are.

Let this be your gentle next step.

Women's Heart Health

Massachusetts General Hospital—Corrigan Women's Heart Health Program
www.massgeneral.org
Focused on clinical care, education, and research in women's cardiovascular disease. Offers holistic, patient-centered support.

SCAD Alliance
www.scadalliance.org
A support organization for patients and families affected by spontaneous coronary artery dissection. Includes medical research, education, and survivor resources.

Go Red for Women/American Heart Association
www.goredforwomen.org
A movement dedicated to raising awareness and saving lives through research, advocacy, and education about women's heart disease.

The Fibromuscular Dysplasia Society of America (FMDSA)
www.fmdsa.org
Dedicated to improving awareness, diagnosis, and treatment of FMD—a rare vascular disease often linked to SCAD. Offers support groups, webinars, and up-to-date research for patients and providers.

Eating Disorders & Body Image

National Eating Disorders Association (NEDA)
www.nationaleatingdisorders.org
Screening tools, treatment access, and community support for those struggling with anorexia, bulimia, binge eating, and disordered eating.

Project HEAL
www.theprojectheal.org
Dedicated to breaking down systemic barriers to eating disorder treatment, especially for marginalized populations. Includes grants and peer support.

PTSD, Panic & Nervous System Healing

National Center for PTSD—U.S. Department of Veterans Affairs
www.ptsd.va.gov
Educational and therapeutic resources for individuals navigating PTSD. Includes self-assessment tools and a PTSD treatment decision aid.

The Trauma Recovery Center Network (TRC)
www.nctsn.org
Local TRCs provide trauma-informed, culturally competent care to survivors of violence and trauma—often at low or no cost.

Crisis Text Line
Text HOME to 741741 | www.crisistextline.org
Free, confidential, 24/7 support via text. A resource for anyone in emotional pain or crisis, any time.

Stay Connected

Ways to Journey Forward Together

This book is just the beginning. You don't have to walk your journey alone.

For free resources, coaching programs, speaking, and heart-led healing:

Visit: www.tarabenoit.com
Follow: @tarabenoitofficial

Scan the QR code below for instant access to all links, downloads, social platforms, and my coaching program.

Let's rise, heal, and keep moving—together.

Acknowledgments

With Gratitude

To my family—
Mom, Dad, Sarah, and David—thank you for holding space for this story to be told. I know it hasn't been easy, and yet you've supported me with grace, strength, and open hearts.

Though the words in these pages are mine, the echoes belong to all of us. Your faith in me, in truth, and in the power of healing for us all— gave me the courage to write what once felt unspeakable.

This book exists because I finally stopped running from the past. But it was your love that gave me the strength to face it. By allowing me to share our story, you've made space for others to feel less alone, and I know, in my heart, that our truth will help others rise.

To Jack—my partner through the unraveling and the rising. Thank you for honoring how much health and movement meant to me, for sharing that same love of strength, and for giving me the space to grow into who I am today.

Maximus and Magnus—you are my why. Your laughter, strength, and light are in every word. Watching you grow into kind, powerful young men gives my life meaning beyond words.

To my extended family—my aunts, uncles, cousins, and the beautiful web of love I was lucky enough to be born into… Thank you. You've shown up for me in quiet ways and loud ones, with laughter, loyalty, and love that spans generations. Your presence has shaped me, grounded me, and lifted me—and this book carries your fingerprints in every chapter.

To my friends—from every chapter of my life—from childhood to high school, from college to yoga mats and gym floors, from neighborhood walks to kid play dates—you've stood beside me in ways words can't always hold. Thank you for the laughter, the late-night texts, and the reminders of who I was when I forgot.

To B and Jenn—you are stitched into my heart and these pages. Thank you for showing up in my hardest seasons with quiet strength and unshakable love.

To Dr. Sarah Tsiaras, Dr. Nandita Scott, and the incredible team at Massachusetts General Hospital—thank you for seeing me, hearing me, and helping me find purpose through pain. Thank you not only for your extraordinary care, but for giving me hope, answers, and a community when I needed it most. Your unwavering dedication to advancing SCAD research and women's heart health has changed my life—and the lives of countless others. I am forever grateful to walk this journey with your expertise, compassion, and advocacy beside me.

To the American Heart Association | Go Red for Women—thank you for giving survivors a voice and for letting me be part of a movement that's changing lives.

To the SCAD survivor community—your strength helped light my way when I couldn't see the path. To the SCAD sisters I've come to know and love—I am writing this book for us. For the stories still unfolding, for the questions we carry, and for the hope that one day we will know more. You are not alone. We are in this together.

To Amberly Lago—my coach, my mentor, the woman who lit the match. Without your guidance, support, and love, this book would still be sitting in my soul, unwritten. You will always hold a special place in my heart. And to the incredible Mastermind women I've met through this journey—your stories, your strength, and your sisterhood have changed my life.

To Cris Cawley and the team at Game Changer Publishing—thank you for holding this vision with care and intention. To every editor, reader, and heart who helped bring this story to life—thank you.

To every person who helped me heal—the therapists who held space, the healers who helped me breathe again, the quiet professionals who offered tools, and the ones who simply listened without judgment—thank you. Your presence was part of the patchwork that held me together when I was coming undone. You may never know the full weight of what you gave me—but I do. And I carry that gratitude in every step forward.

To every person who has ever crossed my path—thank you. I believe we meet each other for a reason.
Some of you offered love. Some offered lessons.
Some stayed for a season, others became part of my soul's fabric.
Each of you helped shape this journey in some way.

To the friends who became family,
to the strangers who offered kindness,
to the hearts that cracked me open—
you are all part of this story.

I believe love doesn't just run through our hearts—
it can move mountains.
And with the right people beside us,
we can heal from anything.

To those who stood with me, loved me, challenged me,
or simply saw me along the way—
thank you. You were part of the becoming.

And to every woman—and every soul—finding themselves in these pages:
I wrote this book for you.
For the parts of you that broke,
and the parts that are still rising.
For the deep knowing that you are never truly alone.

With gratitude, with purpose, with everything I've become—
Thank you for walking this road with me.
The story isn't over. Keep rising.

With love and light,
Tara 🖤

www.ingramcontent.com/pod-product-compliance
Lightning Source LLC
Chambersburg PA
CBHW030248010526
44107CB00031B/1362/J